Be
AVAILABLE

Be
AVAILABLE

WARREN W. WIERSBE

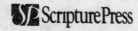ScripturePress

Amersham-on-the-Hill, Bucks HP6 6JQ, England

ISBN 1 872059 90 2

Unless otherwise noted, Scripture quotations are from the
Authorized (King James) Version. Other quotations are from
the *American Standard Version* SCasv),*New American Standard
Bible* (NASB), © the Lockman Foundation 1960, 1962, 1963,
1968, 1971, 1972, 1973, 1975, 1977; the *Holy Bible, New
International Version* (NIV), Copyright © 1973, 1978, 1984 by
International Bible Society. Used by permission of Zondervan
Bible Publishing House. All rights reserved; *The New King
James Version* (NKJV). © 1979, 1980, 1982, Thomas Nelson, Inc.
Publishers; and *The Living Bible* (TLB), © 1971, Tyndale House
Publishers, Wheaton, IL 60189. Used by permission.

Front cover photograph: Images Colour Library

Production and Printing in England for
SCRIPTURE PRESS FOUNDATION (UK) LTD
Raans Road, Amersham-on-the-Hill, Bucks HP6 6JQ by
Nuprint Ltd., Station Road, Harpenden, Herts AL5 4SE

CONTENTS

Preface **7**

1. It Was the Worst of Times (Jud. 1–2) **9**

2. The Weapons of Our Warfare (Jud. 3) **22**

3. "Two Are Better Than One, and Three Are Better Still" (Jud. 4–5) **34**

4. God's Man in Manasseh (Jud. 6) **46**

5. Faith Is the Victory (Jud. 7) **58**

6. Win the War, Lose the Victory (Jud. 8) **69**

7. My Kingdom Come (Jud. 9) **79**

8. Local Reject Makes Good (Jud. 10–12) **90**

9. The Light That Flickered (Jud. 13–14) **104**

10. The Light That Failed (Jud. 15–16) **115**

11. "The Center Cannot Hold" (Jud. 17–18) **128**

12. War and Peace (Jud. 19–21) **139**

13. Looking Back and Looking Around (Drawing Some Lessons from the Book of Judges) **149**

Endnotes **157**

PREFACE

"Straight ahead lies yesterday!"

Dr. Harry Rimmer used to make that statement when referring to biblical history and prophecy; and then he would add, "Future events cast their shadows before them."

In other words, it's all happened before; and philosopher George Santayana was right: "Those who cannot remember the past are condemned to repeat it."

I think that we today are living in a period similar to that described in the Book of Judges

- There is no king in Israel.
- People are doing what is right in their own eyes.
- God's people can't seem to work together.
- People are in bondage to various enemies.

But here and there, God is raising up men and women who believe Him, confront the enemy, and win the victory.

The challenge of the Book of Judges is—be available! No matter how dark the day, God can still work through people who will trust His Word, yield to His Spirit, and do His bidding.

Will you be among them?

Warren W. Wiersbe

A Suggested Outline of the Book of Judges

Theme: Obedience brings God's blessing; disobedience brings
       God's discipline

Theme verse: Judges 21:25 (see also 17:6; 18:1; 19:1)

I. Disobedience: Israel Turns from God—1–2
  1. Early victories—1:1-26
  2. Repeated defeats—1:27-36
  3. National apostasy—2:1-15
  4. Divine mercy—2:16-23

II. Discipline: The Lord Chastens Israel—3–16
  1. Othniel, Ehud, and Shamgar—3
  2. Deborah and Barak—4–5
  3. Gideon—6–8
  4. Abimelech—9
  5. Tola and Jair—10
  6. Jephthah—11:1–12:7
  7. Ibzan, Elon, and Abdon—12:8-15
  8. Samson—13–16

III. Disorder: Israel Sinks into Anarchy—7–21
  1. Religious confusion—17–18
  2. Immorality—19
  3. Civil war—20–21

ONE

It Was the Worst of Times

FAMILY FEUD LEAVES 69 BROTHERS DEAD!

POWERFUL GOVERNMENT LEADER CAUGHT IN "LOVE NEST."

GANG RAPE LEADS TO VICTIM'S DEATH AND DISMEMBERMENT.

GIRLS AT PARTY KIDNAPPED AND FORCED TO MARRY STRANGERS.

WOMAN JUDGE SAYS TRAVELERS NO LONGER SAFE ON HIGHWAYS.

Sensational headlines like these are usually found on the front page of supermarket tabloids, but the above headlines actually describe some of the events narrated in the Book of Judges.[1] What a contrast they are to the closing chapters of the Book of Joshua, where you see a nation resting from war and enjoying the riches God had given them in the Promised Land. But the Book of Judges pictures Israel suffering from invasion, slavery, poverty, and civil war. What happened?

BE AVAILABLE

The nation of Israel quickly decayed after a new generation took over, a generation that knew neither Joshua nor Joshua's God. "And the people served the Lord all the days of Joshua, and all the days of the elders that outlived Joshua, who had seen all the great works of the Lord, that He did for Israel . . . and there arose another generation after them, which knew not the Lord, nor yet the works which He had done for Israel" (Jud. 2:7, 10; and see Josh. 24:31). Instead of exhibiting spiritual fervor, Israel sank into *apathy;* instead of obeying the Lord, the people moved into *apostasy;* and instead of the nation enjoying law and order, the land was filled with *anarchy.* Indeed, for Israel it was the worst of times.

One of the key verses in the Book of Judges is 21:25: "In those days there was no king in Israel; every man did that which was right in his own eyes" (see 17:6; 18:1; 19:1).² At Mt. Sinai, the Lord had taken Israel to be His "kingdom of priests," declaring that He alone would reign over them (Ex. 19:1-8). Moses reaffirmed the kingship of Jehovah when he explained the covenant to the new generation before they entered Canaan (Deut. 29ff). After the conquest of Jericho and Ai, Joshua declared to Israel her kingdom responsibilities (Josh. 8:30-35), and he reminded the people of them again before his death (Josh. 24). Even Gideon, perhaps the greatest of the judges, refused to set up a royal dynasty. "I will not rule over you," he said, "neither shall my son rule over you: the Lord shall rule over you" (Jud. 8:23).

Deuteronomy 6 outlined the nation's basic responsibilities: love and obey Jehovah as the only true God (vv. 1-5); teach your children God's laws (vv. 6-9); be thankful for God's blessings (vv. 10-15); and separate yourself from the worship of the pagan gods in the land of Canaan (vv. 16-25). Unfortunately, the new generation failed in each of those responsibilities. The people didn't want to "seek ye first the kingdom of God, and His righteousness" (Matt. 6:33); they would rather

10

experiment with the idolatry of the godless nations around them. As a result, Israel plunged into moral, spiritual, and political disaster.

One of two things was true: either the older generation had failed to instruct their children and grandchildren in the ways of the Lord, or, if they had faithfully taught them, then the new generation had refused to submit to God's Law and follow God's ways. "Righteousness exalts a nation, but sin is a reproach to any people" (Prov. 14:34, NKJV). The Book of Judges is the record of that reproach, and the first two chapters describe four stages in Israel's decline and fall.

1. Fighting the enemy (Jud. 1:1-21)

The Book of Judges begins with a series of victories and defeats that took place after the death of Joshua. The boundary lines for the twelve tribes had been determined years before (Josh. 13–22), but the people had not yet fully claimed their inheritance by defeating and dislodging the entrenched inhabitants of the land. When Joshua was an old man, the Lord said to him, "You are old, advanced in years, and there remains very much land yet to be possessed" (Josh. 13:1, NKJV). The people of Israel *owned* all the land, but they didn't *possess* all of it; and therefore they couldn't *enjoy* all of it.

The victories of Judah (vv. 1-20). Initially the people of Israel wisely sought God's guidance and asked the Lord which tribe was to engage the enemy first. Perhaps God told Judah to go first because Judah was the kingly tribe (Gen. 49:8-9). Judah believed God's promise, obeyed God's counsel, and even asked the people of the tribe of Simeon to go to battle with them. Since Leah had given birth to Judah and Simeon, these tribes were blood brothers (Gen. 35:23). Incidentally, Simeon actually had its inheritance within the tribe of Judah (Josh. 19:1).

When Joshua was Israel's leader, all the tribes worked

together in obeying the will of God. In the Book of Judges, however, you don't find the nation working together as a unit. When God needed someone to deliver His people, He called that person out of one of the tribes and told him or her what to do. In obedience to the Lord, Moses had appointed Joshua as his successor; but later God didn't command Joshua to name a successor. These circumstances somewhat parallel the situation of the church in the world today. Unfortunately, God's people aren't working together to defeat the enemy; but here and there, God is raising up men and women of faith who are experiencing His blessing and power and are leading His people to victory.

With God's help, the two tribes conquered the Canaanites at *Bezek* (Jud. 1:4-7), captured, humiliated, and incapacitated one of their kings by cutting off his thumbs and big toes. (See Jud. 16:21; 1 Sam. 11:2; and 2 Kings 25:7 for further instances about being disabled.) With those handicaps, he wouldn't be able to run easily or use a weapon successfully. Thus the "lord of Bezek" was paid back for what he had done to seventy other kings, although he may have been exaggerating a bit when he made this claim.

Those seventy kings illustrate the sad plight of anybody who has given in to the enemy: they couldn't walk or run correctly; they couldn't use a sword effectively; they were in the place of humiliation instead of on the throne; and they were living on scraps and leftovers instead of feasting at the table. What a difference it makes when you live by faith and reign in life through Jesus Christ (Rom. 10:17).

Jerusalem (Jud. 1:8) was Israel's next trophy; but though the Israelites conquered the city, they didn't occupy it (v. 21). That wasn't done until the time of David (2 Sam. 5:7). Judah and Benjamin were neighboring tribes; and since the city was located on their border, both tribes were involved in attacking it (Josh. 15:63). Later, Jerusalem would become "the city of

David" and the capital of Israel.

They next attacked the area south and west of Jerusalem, which included *Hebron* (Jud. 1:9-10, 20) This meant fighting in the hill country, the south (Negev), and the foothills. Joshua had promised Hebron to Caleb because of his faithfulness to the Lord at Kadesh-Barnea (Num. 13-14; Josh. 14:6-15; Deut. 1:34-36). Sheshai, Ahiman, and Talmai were descendants of the giant Anak whose people had frightened ten of the twelve Jewish spies who first explored the land (Num. 13:22, 28). Even though Caleb and Joshua, the other two spies, had the faith needed to overcome the enemy, the people wouldn't listen to them.

Faith must have run in Caleb's family, because the city of *Debir* (Jud. 1:11-16)[3] was taken by Othniel, Caleb's nephew (3:9; Josh. 15:17). For a reward, he received Caleb's daughter Acsah as his wife. Othniel later was called to serve as Israel's first judge (Jud. 3:7-11). Since water was a precious commodity, and land was almost useless without it, Acsah urged her husband to ask her father to give them the land containing the springs that they needed. Apparently Othniel was better at capturing cities than he was at asking favors from his father-in-law, so Acsah had to do it herself. Her father then gave her the upper and lower springs. Perhaps this extra gift was related in some way to her dowry.

The Kenites (1:16) were an ancient people (Gen. 15:19) who are thought to have been nomadic metal workers. (The Hebrew word *qayin* means "a metalworker, a smith.") According to Judges 4:11, the Kenites were descended from Moses' brother-in-law Hobab,[4] and thus were allies of Israel. The city of palms was Jericho, a deserted and condemned city (Josh. 6:26), so the Kenites moved to another part of the land under the protection of the tribe of Judah.

After Judah and Simeon destroyed *Hormah* (Jud. 1:17), the army of Judah turned its attention to the Philistine cities of

Gaza, Ashkelon, and Ekron (vv. 18-19). Because the Philistines had iron chariots, the Jews couldn't easily defeat them on level ground, but they did claim the hill country.

What is important about the military history is that "the Lord was with Judah" (v. 19), and that's what gave them victory. (See Num. 14:42-43; Josh. 1:5 and 6:27; and Jud. 6:16.) "If God be for us, who can be against us?" (Rom. 8:31)

The victory of Joseph (vv. 22-26). The tribe of Ephraim joined with the western section of the tribe of Manasseh and, with the Lord's help, they took the city of Bethel. This city was important to the Jews because of its connection with the patriarchs (Gen. 12:8; 13:3; 28:10-12; 35:1-7). Apparently it hadn't been taken during the Conquest under Joshua, or if it had been, the Jews must have lost control. The saving of the informer's family reminds us of the salvation of Rahab's family when Jericho was destroyed (Josh. 2, 6). How foolish of this rescued people not to stay with the Israelites, where they were safe and could learn about the true and living God.

2. Sparing the enemy (Jud. 1:21, 27-36)

Benjamin, Ephraim, Manasseh, Zebulun, Asher, Naphtali, and Dan all failed to overcome the enemy and had to allow these godless nations to continue living in their tribal territories. The enemy even chased the tribe of Dan out of the plains into the mountains! The Jebusites remained in Jerusalem (v. 21), and the Canaanites who remained were finally pressed "into forced labor" when the Jews became stronger (v. 28, NIV). Eventually Solomon conscripted these Canaanite peoples to build the temple (1 Kings 9:20-22; 2 Chron. 8:7-8), but this was no compensation for the problems the Canaanites caused the Jews. This series of tribal defeats was the first indication that Israel was no longer walking by faith and trusting God to give them victory.

The priests possessed a copy of the Book of Deuteronomy

and were commanded to read it publicly to the nation every Sabbatical Year during the Feast of Tabernacles (Deut. 31:9-13). Had they been faithful to do their job, the spiritual leaders would have read Deuteronomy 7 and warned the Israelites not to spare their pagan neighbors. The priests also would have reminded the people of God's promises that He would help them defeat their enemies (Deut. 31:1-8). It was by receiving and obeying the Book of the Law that Joshua had grown in faith and courage (Josh. 1:1-9; Rom. 10:17), and that same Word would have enabled the new generation to overcome their enemies and claim their inheritance.

The first step the new generation took toward defeat and slavery was *neglecting the Word of God,* and generations ever since have made that same mistake. "For the time will come when they will not endure sound doctrine, but according to their own desires, because they have itching ears, they will heap up for themselves teachers; and they will turn their ears away from the truth, and be turned aside to fables" (2 Tim. 4:3-4, NKJV). I fear that too many believers today are trying to live on religious fast-food dispensed for easy consumption (no chewing necessary) by entertaining teachers who give people what they want, not what they need. Is it any wonder many churches aren't experiencing God's power at work in their ministries?

But wasn't it cruel and unjust for God to *command* Israel to exterminate the nations in Canaan? Not in the least! To begin with, He had been patient with these nations for centuries and had mercifully withheld His judgment (Gen. 15:16; 2 Peter 3:9). Their society, and especially their religion, was unspeakably wicked (Rom. 1:18ff) and should have been wiped out years before Israel appeared on the scene.

Something else is true: These nations had been warned by the judgments God had inflicted on others, especially on Egypt and the nations east of the Jordan (Josh. 2:8-13). Rahab and her family had sufficient information to be able to repent and believe, and God saved them (Josh. 2; 6:22-25). Therefore, we have every right to conclude that God would have saved anybody who had turned to Him. These nations were sinning against a flood of light in rejecting God's truth and going their own way.

God didn't want the filth of the Canaanite society and religion to contaminate His people Israel. Israel was God's special people, chosen to fulfill divine purposes in this world. Israel would give the world the knowledge of the true God, the Holy Scriptures, and the Savior. In order to accomplish God's purposes, the nation had to be separated from all other nations; for if Israel was polluted, how could the Holy Son of God come into the world? "God is perpetually at war with sin," wrote G. Campbell Morgan. "That is the whole explanation of the extermination of the Canaanites."[5]

The main deity in Canaan was Baal, god of rainfall[6] and fertility, and Ashtoreth was his spouse. If you wanted to have fruitful orchards and vineyards, flourishing crops, and increasing flocks and herds, you worshiped Baal by visiting a temple prostitute. This combination of idolatry, immorality, and agricultural success was difficult for men to resist, which explains why God told Israel to wipe out the Canaanite religion completely (Num. 33:51-56; Deut. 7:1-5).

3. Imitating the enemy (Jud. 2:1-13)

The danger. In this day of "pluralism," when society contains people of opposing beliefs and lifestyles, it's easy to get confused and start thinking that *tolerance* is the same as *approval.* It isn't. In a democracy, the law gives people the freedom to worship as they please; and I must exercise patience and tolerance with those who believe and practice things that I feel God has condemned in His Word. The church today doesn't wield the sword (Rom. 13) and therefore it has no authority to eliminate people who disagree with the Christian faith. But we do have the obligation before God to maintain a separate walk so we won't become defiled by those who disagree with us (2 Cor. 6:14–7:1). We must seek by prayer, witness, and loving persuasion to win those to Christ who as yet haven't trusted Him.

The Jews eventually became so accustomed to the sinful ways of their pagan neighbors that those ways didn't seem sinful any more. The Jews then became interested in how their neighbors worshiped, until finally Israel started to live like their enemies and imitate their ways. For believers today, the first step away from the Lord is "friendship with the world" (James 4:4, NKJV), which then leads to our being spotted by the world (1:27). The next step is to "love the world" (1 John 2:15) and gradually become "conformed to this world" (Rom. 12:2). This can lead to being "condemned with the world" (1 Cor. 11:32), the kind of judgment that came to Lot (Gen. 19), Samson (Jud. 16), and Saul (1 Sam. 15, 31).

The disobedience (vv. 2:1-5). In the Old Testament, the "angel of the Lord" is generally interpreted to be the Lord Himself, who occasionally came to earth (a theophany) to deliver an important message. It was probably the Lord Jesus Christ, the second Person of the Godhead, in a temporary preincarnation appearance. (See Gen. 16:9; 22:11; 48:16; Ex. 3:2; Jud. 6:11 and 13:3; 2 Kings 19:35.) The fact that God Himself came to give the message shows how serious things had become in Israel.

The tabernacle was originally located at Gilgal (Josh. 4:19-20), and it was there that the men of Israel were circumcised and "rolled away" the reproach of Egypt (Josh. 5:2-9). It was also there that the Lord appeared to Joshua and assured him of victory as he began his campaign to conquer Canaan (Josh. 5:13-15). To Joshua, the angel of the Lord brought a message of encouragement; but to the new generation described in the

Book of Judges, He brought a message of punishment.

The Lord had kept His covenant with Israel; not one word of His promises had failed (Josh. 23:5, 10, 15; 1 Kings 8:56). He had asked them to keep their covenant with Him by obeying His law and destroying the Canaanite religious system—their altars, temples, and idols. (In Ex. 23:20-25, note the association between the angel of the Lord and the command to destroy the false religion; and see also Ex. 34:10-17 and Deut. 7:1-11.) But Israel disobeyed the Lord and not only spared the Canaanites and their godless religious system but also began to follow the enemy's lifestyle themselves.

In His covenant, God promised to bless Israel if the people obeyed Him and to discipline them if they disobeyed Him (see Deut. 27–28). *God is always faithful to His Word, whether in blessing us or chastening us; for in both, He displays His integrity and His love (Heb. 12:1-11).* God would prefer to bestow the positive blessings of life that bring us enjoyment, but He doesn't hesitate to remove those blessings if our suffering will motivate us to return to Him in repentance.

By their disobedience, the nation of Israel made it clear that they wanted the Canaanites to remain in the land. God let them have their way (Ps. 106:15), but He warned them of the tragic consequences. The nations in the land of Canaan would become *thorns* that would afflict Israel and *traps* that would ensnare them. Israel would look to the Canaanites for pleasures but would only experience pain; they would rejoice in their freedom only to see that freedom turn into their bondage.[7]

No wonder the people wept when they heard the message! (The Hebrew word *bochim* means "weepers.") However, their sorrow was because of the *consequences* of their sins and not because the wickedness of their sins had *convicted* them. It was a shallow and temporary sorrow that never led them to true repentance (2 Cor. 7:8-11).

4. Obeying the enemy (Jud. 2:6-23)

The sin in our lives that we fail to conquer will even
conquer us. The people of Israel found themselves enslaved
to one pagan nation after another as the Lord kept His word
and chastened His people. Consider the sins of that new
generation.

They forgot what the Lord had done (vv. 6-10). At that point
in Israel's history, Joshua stood next to Moses as a great
hero, and yet the new generation didn't recognize who he
was or what he had done. In his popular novel *1984,* George
Orwell wrote, "Who controls the past controls the future:
who controls the present controls the past." Once they got in
control of the present, both Hitler and Stalin rewrote past
history so they could control future events; and for a time it
worked. How important it is for each new generation to recognize and appreciate the great men and women who helped
to build and protect their nation! It's disturbing when "revi-
sionist" historians debunk the heroes and heroines of the
past and almost make them criminals.

They forsook what the Lord had said (vv. 11-13). Had they
remembered Joshua, they would have known his "farewell
speeches" given to the leaders and the people of Israel (Josh.
23–24). Had they known those speeches, they would have
known the Law of Moses; for in his final messages, Joshua
emphasized the covenant God had made with Israel and the
responsibility Israel had to keep it. When you forget the
Word of God, you are in danger of forsaking the God of the
Word, which explains why Israel turned to the vile and vicious worship of Baal.

They forfeited what the Lord had promised (vv. 14-15). When
they went out to fight their enemies, Israel was defeated,
because the Lord wasn't with His people. This is what Moses
had said would happen (Deut. 28:25-26); but that isn't all:
Israel's enemies eventually became their masters! God permit-

ted one nation after another to invade the Promised Land and enslave His people, making life so miserable for them that they cried out for help. Had the Jews obeyed the Lord, their armies would have been victorious; but left to themselves, they were defeated and humiliated.

They failed to learn from what the Lord did (vv. 16-23). Whenever Israel turned away from the Lord to worship idols, He chastened them severely; and when in their misery they turned back to Him, He liberated them. But just as soon as they were free and their situation was comfortable again, Israel went right back into the same old sins. "And the Children of Israel did evil in the sight of the Lord. . . . Therefore the anger of the Lord was hot against Israel, and He sold them into the hand of . . ." is the oft-repeated statement that records the sad cyclical nature of Israel's sins (3:7-8, see also v. 12; 4:1-4; 6:1; 10:6-7; 13:1). The people wasted their suffering. They didn't learn the lessons God wanted them to learn and profit from His chastening.

God delivered His people by raising up judges, who defeated the enemy and set Israel free. The Hebrew word translated "judge" means "to save, to rescue." The judges were deliverers who won great military victories with the help of the Lord. But the judges were also leaders who helped the people settle their disputes (4:4-5). The judges came from different tribes and functioned locally rather than nationally; and in some cases, their terms of office overlapped. The word "judge" is applied to only eight of the twelve people we commonly call "judges," but all of them functioned as counselors and deliverers. The eight men are: Othniel (3:9), Tola (10:1-2), Jair (10:3-5), Jephthah (11), Ibzan (12:8-10), Elon (12:11-12), Abdon (12:13-15), and Samson (15:20; 16:31).

The cycle of disobedience, discipline, despair, and deliverance is seen today whenever God's people turn away from His Word and go their own way. *If disobedience isn't followed*

20

by divine discipline, then the person is not truly a child of God; for God chastens all of His children (Heb. 12:3-13). God has great compassion for His people, but He is angry at their sins.

The Book of Judges is the inspired record of Israel's failures and God's faithfulness. But if we study this book only as past history, we'll miss the message completely. *This book is about God's people today.* When the psalmist reviewed the period of the Judges (Ps. 106:40-46), he concluded with a prayer that we need to pray today: "Save us, O Lord our God, and gather us from the nations, that we may give thanks to Your holy name and glory in Your praise" (Ps. 106:47, NIV).

T W O

The Weapons of Our Warfare

The weapons we fight with are not the weapons of the world."

That statement could have been made by a space alien in a sci-fi novel, but it wasn't. The Apostle Paul wrote those words to the believers in Corinth (2 Cor. 10:4, NIV), reminding them of a principle every Christian needs to take to heart: *When God goes to war, He usually chooses the most unlikely soldiers, hands them the most unusual weapons, and accomplishes through them the most unpredictable results.*

For example, God gave Shamgar an ox goad, and with it he killed 600 men (3:31). Jael used a hammer and tent peg to kill a captain (4:21), and Gideon routed the whole Midianite army with only pitchers and torches as weapons (7:20). Samson slaughtered 1,000 Philistines using the jawbone of an ass (15:15), and young David killed the giant Goliath with a stone hurled from a shepherd's sling (1 Sam. 17). West Point isn't likely to offer courses on how to use these weapons.

Though our world has changed dramatically since the days of the Judges, the "world system" is still the same because human nature hasn't changed (1 John 2:15-17). As long as we're in this world, God's people are involved in a spiritual battle against Satan and his armies (Eph. 6:10-19), and God is still looking for men and women who have what it takes to win: power, strategy, and courage. These three essentials for victory are illustrated in this chapter in the lives of the first three judges.

1. Othniel: the power of God (Jud. 3:1-11)

In this chapter, you will find "five lords of the Philistines" (v. 3) and the King of Moab called "lord" (v. 25); but more importantly "the Lord," meaning Jehovah God, is named fifteen times in these thirty verses. That lets us know who is really in charge. The Presbyterian missionary leader A.T. Pierson used to say that "history is His story," and he was right. As He executes His divine decrees, God never violates human responsibility, but He does rule and overrule in the affairs of individuals and nations to accomplish His great purposes on this earth.

The early church prayed, "Lord, You *are* God!" and they gladly confessed that their enemies could do only "whatever Your hand and Your purpose determined before to be done" (Acts 4:24, 28, NKJV). Poet T.S. Eliot said, "Destiny waits in the hand of God, not in the hands of statesmen."

God's mercy toward His people (vv. 1-4). The tribe of Judah was not able to hold on to the key Philistine cities they had taken (1:18; 3:3); and as we saw in chapter 1, the other tribes failed to conquer the Canaanite nations. These surviving nations adopted a "good neighbor" policy toward Israel that eventually defeated Israel from within. Sometimes Satan comes as a lion to devour, but often he comes as a serpent to deceive (1 Peter 5:8; 2 Cor. 11:3).

God could have judged Israel for sparing the wicked Canaanite nations, but in His mercy He spared them because He had purposes for them to fulfill. Israel had committed a serious blunder in not trusting God to give them victory, but

God sought to use their mistake for their own good. Romans 8:28 worked even in Old Testament days.

He would use the enemy *to train Israel*, to help the new generation learn the meaning of war (Jud. 3:1-2; see Ex. 13:17). Life had been relatively easy for the Jews in the Promised Land, and they needed the challenge of ever-present danger to keep them alert and disciplined. This is not to say God always approves of war or that participating in conflict always builds character. Combat experience might do just the opposite. The point is that the Jews had to keep some kind of standing army, or their enemies could quickly unite and overpower them, especially when Israel was at such a low ebb spiritually. In the years to come, both Saul and David would need effective armies in order to overcome their many enemies and establish the kingdom.

God also used the Canaanite nations *to test Israel* and reveal whether or not His people would obey the regulations Moses had given them from the Lord (Jud. 3:4). God had made it very clear to the Jews that they were not to study "comparative religion" and get interested in the pagan practices of the Canaanites (Deut. 7:1-11). It was that kind of curiosity that had brought divine judgment on Israel in the land of Moab (see Num. 25), because curiosity is often the first step toward conformity.

Of course, Israel should have been a witness to the surviving pagan nations and sought to win them to faith in the true and living God, but they failed in that responsibility as well. What a difference it would have made in subsequent national history if the Jews had won the Canaanites to the Lord instead of the Canaanites winning the Jews to Baal!

God's anger toward His people (vv. 5-8). God had put a wall between Israel and her neighbors, not because Israel was *better* than any other nation, but because she was *different*. Instead of worshiping idols, the Jews worshiped the one true

God who made the heavens and the earth. Humans did not devise the laws and covenants of Israel; God did. Israel alone had the true sanctuary, where God dwelt in His glory; it was the true priesthood, ordained by God; and it had the true altar and sacrifices that God would respect (Rom. 9:4-5). Only through Israel would all the nations of the earth be blessed (Gen. 12:1-3).

When Israel obeyed the Lord, He blessed them richly; *and both their conduct and God's blessing were a testimony to their unbelieving neighbors.* (See Gen. 23:6; 26:26-33; 30:27; 39:5.) The pagan people would say, "These Jews are different! The God they worship and serve is a great God!" And the Jewish people would then have had opportunities to tell their neighbors how to trust Jehovah and receive His forgiveness and blessing. (See Deut. 4:1-13.)

Alas, instead of trusting God to change their neighbors, the gods of their neighbors changed the Jews; and everything Moses warned them not to do, they did. The Jews broke down the wall of separation between themselves and their godless neighbors, and the results were tragic. Contrary to God's law, Jewish men married pagan wives, and Jewish women married pagan husbands (Gen. 24:3; 26:34-35; 27:46; Ex. 34:15-16; Deut. 7:3-4; Josh. 23:12). The idolaters gradually stole the hearts of their mates from worshiping Jehovah to worshiping false gods. King Solomon made this same mistake. After all, when you marry outside the will of God, you have to do something to keep peace in the family! (See 1 Kings 11:1-13; 2 Cor. 6:14–7:1.)

Is it any wonder that God became angry?[1] Is it any wonder He humiliated Israel by using pagan nations to discipline His own people? Since Israel was acting like the pagans, God had to treat them like pagans! "To the faithful you show yourself faithful, to the blameless you show yourself blameless, to the pure you show yourself pure, but to the crooked you show yourself shrewd" (Ps. 18:25-26, NIV).

Jehovah is the God of all the nations, "for dominion belongs to the Lord and He rules over the nations" (Ps. 22:27-28, NIV). Proud King Nebuchadnezzar had to learn the hard way "that the Most High rules in the kingdom of men, and gives it to whomever He chooses" (Dan. 4:25, NKJV).

Four times in the Book of Judges we're told that God "sold" His people to the enemy (2:14; 3:8; 4:2; 10:7; and see 1 Sam. 12:9; 1 Kings 21:20, 25; Ps. 44:12). The Jews acted like slaves, so God sold them like slaves. Had the Jews been faithful to the Lord, He would have sold their enemies into Israel's hands (Deut. 32:30).

The name of the King of Mesopotamia means "doubly wicked Cushan," which may have been a nickname that his enemies gave him. We aren't told where he invaded Israel, although logically the attack would have come from the north; nor are we told how much of the land he subjugated for those eight painful years. Since the deliverer God raised up was from Judah, it's possible that the invading army had penetrated that far south in Israel when the Lord decided to intervene on behalf of His suffering people.

Charles Spurgeon said that God never allows His people to sin successfully. Their sin will either destroy them or it will invite the chastening hand of God. If the history of Israel teaches the contemporary church anything it's the obvious lesson that "righteousness exalts a nation, but sin is a disgrace to any people" (Prov. 14:34, NIV).

God's salvation for His people (vv. 9-11). There's no evidence that the people repented of their sins when they cried out to God for help, but the Lord responded to their plight and gave them a deliverer. It was the Exodus experience all over again: "And God heard their groaning, and God remembered His covenant with Abraham, with Isaac, and with Jacob. And God looked upon the Children of Israel, and God had respect unto them" (Ex. 2:24-25). The word "knew" means much more than intellectual understanding, for God knows everything. It means that God identified with their trials and felt a concern for their welfare.

The deliverer He raised up was Othniel, the man who captured Hebron and married Caleb's daughter (1:10-13). Bible scholars don't agree as to the exact blood relationship Othniel had to Caleb. Was Othniel Caleb's nephew—that is, the son of Kenaz, Caleb's younger brother—or was he simply Caleb's younger brother? As far as the text is concerned, either interpretation is possible.

If he was Caleb's brother, then why was his father's name Kenaz instead of Jephunneh? (1 Chron. 4:13; Josh. 14:6) Perhaps Jephunneh had died, and Caleb's mother married Kenaz and gave birth to Othniel. Thus, Othniel would have been Caleb's half-brother. First Chronicles 4:13 indicates that Othniel was the *son* of Kenaz, but the word "son" is used rather broadly in Jewish genealogies and doesn't always mean a direct father/son relationship.

Fortunately, we don't have to untangle the branches in Othniel's family tree before we can benefit from the example of his life and ministry. By blood and by marriage, he belonged to a family noted for its courageous faith and its willingness to face the enemy and depend on God for the victory. When God called Othniel, he was available for the Lord, and the Spirit of the Lord came upon him and empowered him for battle (Jud. 3:10).

" 'Not by might nor by power, but by My Spirit.' says the Lord of hosts" (Zech. 4:6, NKJV). This was the secret of Othniel's strength, as it was with Gideon (Jud. 6:34), Jephthah (11:29) and Samson (14:6, 19; 15:14); and it must be the source of the believer's power today (Acts 1:8; 2:4; 4:8, 31; Eph. 5:18). One of the former directors of The Evangelical Alliance Mission, T.J. Bach, said, "The Holy Spirit longs to reveal to you the deeper things of God. He longs to love through you. He longs to work through you. Through the blessed Holy Spirit you may have: strength for every duty, wisdom for every problem, comfort in every sorrow, joy in His overflowing service."

Othniel not only rescued his nation from bondage, but also served his people as judge for forty years. This meant that he exercised authority in managing the affairs of the nation, and it was his spiritual and civil leadership that brought rest to the land. *Never underestimate the good that one person can do who is filled with the Spirit of God and obedient to the will of God.*

2. Ehud: effective strategy (Jud. 3:12-30)

Unlike Moses, who appointed Joshua to lead Israel, the judges didn't have the authority to name a successor. When God called men and women to serve as judges, they obeyed, did His work, and then passed from the scene. One would hope that their godly influence would make a lasting difference in the spiritual life of the nation, but such wasn't the case. No sooner was a judge off the scene than the people were back to worshiping Baal and forsaking the Lord.

You would think that gratitude alone would have motivated the people of Israel to obey the Lord and be faithful to His covenant, especially after enduring eight years of painful servitude. And think of all that God had done for Israel in the past! They would have been a forgotten little nation if God hadn't loved them and chosen them for Himself (Deut. 7:1-11). They would have perished in Egypt or in the wilderness if God hadn't delivered them and cared for them. They would have died on the battlefields of Canaan if the Lord hadn't given them victory over their enemies. They would have been wallowing in moral sewage if the Lord hadn't given them His Law and the priests to teach it to them. They had

God's presence in the tabernacle and God's promises in the covenant, so what more could they want?

Somewhere the system broke down, and I think it was with the priests and the parents. The priests and Levites were not only to officiate at the tabernacle, but they also were to teach the Law to the people and encourage them to obey it (Lev. 10:11; Deut. 33:8-10; 17:8-9; 1 Sam. 2:12-17; Mal. 2:1-9). Jewish parents were expected to teach their children the ways of the Lord (Deut. 6:6-25; 11:18-21; and see Gen. 18:17-19 and Job 1:5) and be good examples for them to follow. During the period of the Judges, however, it appears that the older generation neglected the important ministry of instructing the new generation about the fear of the Lord (Ps. 34:11).

Eglon, the oppressor (vv. 12-14). The armies of Mesopotamia came a long distance to invade Israel; but the Moabites, Ammonites, and Amalekites were not only neighbors but also *relatives* of the Jews. Lot, the nephew of Abraham, was the ancestor of Moab and Ammon (Gen. 19:30-38); and Esau, the brother of Jacob, was the ancestor of Amalek (Gen. 36:12, 16; Deut. 25:17, 19).

Eglon, the King of Moab, organized the confederacy and set up his headquarters at Jericho, "the city of palm trees" (Deut. 34:3). Jericho was under a curse (Josh. 6:26), and there's no evidence that the city had been rebuilt; but the location was ideal for directing military operations, and there was an abundance of water there. For eighteen years, Eglon and his allies made life miserable for the Jews. It must have been especially galling to them to be under the heels of blood relatives who were also their longtime adversaries.

Ehud, the deliverer (vv. 15-30). Othniel, the first judge, had come from the tribe of Judah. The second judge, Ehud, a left-handed man, came from Judah's neighbor, Benjamin — the name "Benjamin" means "son of my right hand." (The

Benjamites were known for their ambidexterity. See Jud. 20:16 and 1 Chron. 12:2.) However, the text of Judges 3:15 can be translated "a man handicapped in the right hand," which suggests that he was not ambidextrous at all but able to use *only* his left hand. If that indeed is the meaning of the text, then Ehud's plan for killing Eglon was a masterpiece of strategy. It's also a great encouragement to people with physical disabilities who may have the erroneous idea that God can't use them in His service.

Ehud had several problems to solve, and he solved them successfully. At the top of the list was how to gain access to King Eglon without making anybody suspicious. He accomplished this by making himself the leader of the commission that brought the king his annual tribute. The paying of tribute not only added to the king's wealth, which he would enjoy, but it also acknowledged the king's authority over Israel; and Eglon would enjoy that as well. Of course, Eglon didn't know that Ehud was God's appointed leader to deliver Israel; otherwise, he would have had him killed on sight.

The second problem was securing a private audience with the king without exciting the distrust of his attendants and guards. Ehud did this first by leaving the king's presence together with his men after they had done homage to Eglon, and then Ehud coming back later *alone* as though he had an urgent message for the king. A solitary man with a lame right hand couldn't be much of a threat to a powerful king, and perhaps this despised Jew really did have a word from his God. Eglon may have felt proud that the God of Israel had a message for him; and since he was no doubt afraid not to listen to it, he dismissed his guards and attendants and gave Ehud a personal interview in his private chambers.

Since Ehud had to kill Eglon in a way that was quick and quiet and that would catch the king by surprise,[2] he made use of his disability. Ehud made a very sharp dagger and hid it under his clothing on his right side. Even if the guards frisked him, they would most likely examine the left side of his body where most men carried their weapons. Seeing that he was a handicapped man, they probably didn't examine him at all.

Even a king must stand to receive a message from God. When Eglon stood, Ehud may have gestured with his right hand to distract him and show him there was nothing in his hand; and then Ehud reached for his dagger and plunged it into the fat king's body. It must have been a powerful thrust because the point of the dagger came out the king's back; and Eglon was dead instantly.[3]

The next problem was how to escape from the palace without getting caught, and this he accomplished by locking the door of the private chamber and delaying the discovery of the corpse. As Ehud hastened away, the attendants concluded that the interview was over; so they went to see if their king wanted anything. The three "behold" statements in verses 24-25 indicate the three surprises that they experienced: the doors were locked, the king didn't respond to their knocks and calls, and the king was dead. All of this took time and gave Ehud opportunity to escape.

His final problem was to rally the troops and attack the enemy. The trumpet signal called the men out, and he led them to the fords of the Jordan, assuring them that the Lord had given Moab into their hands. The victory would come by trusting the Lord and not by depending on their own strength. By guarding the fords, the Israelites prevented the Moabites from escaping or from bringing in fresh troops. Since Ephraim was one of the most powerful tribes in Israel, Ehud had excellent soldiers to command. Accordingly, they killed 10,000 of the best Moabite soldiers. Not only was Moab defeated, but also the tables were turned and the Moabites became subject to Israel. We assume that Moab's defeat was the signal for their allies Ammon and Amalek to leave the field of battle.

If the Jews had been asked to vote on a leader, Ehud probably would have lost on the first ballot. But he was God's choice, and God used him to set the nation free. Moses was slow of speech and Paul was not imposing in his appearance, but Moses and Paul, like Ehud, were men of faith who led others to victory. Ehud turned a disability into a possibility because he depended on the Lord.

3. Shamgar: persistent courage (Jud. 3:31).

Only one verse is devoted to Shamgar and it isn't even stated that he was a judge. Judges 5:6-7 indicates that he was contemporary with Deborah and Barak. "Son of Anath" may mean that he was from the town of Beth Anath in Naphtali (1:33), which was also the tribe Barak came from (4:6; see 5:18). Since Anath was the name of a Canaanite goddess of war, perhaps "son of Anath" was a nickname that meant "son of battle"—that is, a mighty warrior.

What was significant about Shamgar was the weapon that he used. An ox goad was a strong pole about eight feet long. At one end was a sharp metal point for prodding the oxen and at the other end a spade for cleaning the dirt off the plow. It was the closest thing Shamgar could find to a spear because the enemy had confiscated the weapons of the Israelites (5:8; see 1 Sam. 13:19-22).

Here was a man who obeyed God and defeated the enemy even though his resources were limited. Instead of complaining about not possessing a sword or spear, Shamgar gave what he had to the Lord, and the Lord used it. Joseph Parker said, "What is a feeble instrument in the hands of one man is a mighty instrument in the hands of another, simply because the spirit of that other burns with holy determination to accomplish the work that has to be done."[4]

32

Shamgar may have killed all 600 Philistines at one time in one place (see 2 Sam. 8:8-12), but it's also possible that 600 is a cumulative total. An ox goad would be an unwieldy weapon to use if 600 soldiers had attacked Shamgar at one time. Since we don't know the details, we must not speculate. It's just encouraging to know that God enabled him to overcome the enemy though his resources were limited.

The few words that are recorded about Shamgar give me the impression that he was a man of persistent courage, which, of course was born out of his faith in the Lord. To stand his ground against the enemy, having only a farmer's tool instead of a soldier's full military equipment, marks Shamgar out as a brave man with steadfast courage.

Charles Spurgeon once gave a lecture at his Pastor's College entitled "To Workers with Slender Apparatus." Shamgar didn't hear that lecture, but I'm sure he could have given it! And I suspect he would have closed his lecture by saying, "Give whatever tools you have to the Lord, stand your ground courageously, and trust God to use what's in your hand to accomplish great things for His glory."

To paraphrase E.M. Bounds, the world is looking for better methods, but God is looking for better men and women who understand the basics: the power of the Holy Spirit, wise strategy, and steadfast courage.

Othniel, Ehud, and Shamgar have shown us the way. Will we follow?

"Two Are Better than One, and Three Are Better Still"

The cast of characters in this drama is as follows:

Jabin: King of Hazor in Canaan; a tyrant
Deborah: a Jewish judge; a woman of faith and courage
Barak: a reluctant Jewish general
Sisera: captain of Jabin's army
Heber: a Kenite neighbor, at peace with Jabin
Jael: wife of Heber; handy with a hammer
Jehovah God: in charge of wars and weather

Now let the drama unfold.

1. Act one: a tragic situation (Jud. 4:1-3)

Jabin is the key person in act one, for God raised him up to discipline the people of Israel. For eighty years, the Jews had enjoyed rest because of the leadership of Ehud, the longest period of peace recorded in the Book of Judges.[1] But no sooner was this godly judge removed than the people lapsed back into idolatry, and God had to punish them (Jud. 2:10-19).

Israel as portrayed in the Book of Judges illustrates the difference between "religious reformation" and "spiritual revival." Reformation temporarily changes outward conduct while revival permanently alters inward character. When Ehud removed the idols and commanded the people to worship only Jehovah, they obeyed him; but when that constraint was removed, the people obeyed their own desires. The nation of Israel was like the man in Jesus' parable who got rid of one demon, cleaned house, and then ended up with seven worse demons (Matt. 12:43-45). The empty heart is prey to every form of evil.

Canaan was made up of a number of city-states, each of which was ruled by a king (see Josh. 12). "Jabin" was the official title or name of the King of Hazor (Josh. 11:1). He was also called "King of Canaan." This title probably means that he was the head of a confederacy of kings. Joshua had burned Hazor (Josh. 11:13), but the Canaanites had rebuilt it and occupied it. With his large army and his 900 chariots of iron, Jabin was securely in control of the land. As you read the narrative, however, you get the impression that Sisera, captain of Jabin's army, was the real power in the land. Jabin isn't even mentioned in Deborah's song in Judges 5!

Once again, the people of Israel cried out to God, not to forgive their sins but to relieve their suffering. (See vv. 6-8 for a hint of what life was like in those days.) Had they truly repented, God would have done much more than deliver them from physical slavery. He would have liberated them from their spiritual bondage as well. To ask God for comfort and not cleansing is only to sow seeds of selfishness that will eventually produce another bitter harvest. David's prayer is what Israel needed to pray: "Create in me a clean heart, O God; and renew a right spirit within me" (Ps. 51:10).

2. Act two: a divine revelation (Jud. 4:4-7)

God had raised up a courageous woman named Deborah ("bee") to be the judge in the land. This was an act of grace, but it was also an act of humiliation for the Jews; for they lived in a male-dominated society that wanted only mature male leadership. "As for My people, children are their oppressors, and women rule over them" (Isa. 3:12). For God to give His people a woman judge was to treat them like little children, which is exactly what they were when it came to spiritual things.[2]

Deborah was both a judge and a prophetess. Moses' sister Miriam was a prophetess (Ex. 15:20); and later biblical history introduces us to Huldah (2 Kings 22:14), Noadiah (Neh. 6:14), Anna (Luke 2:36), and the four daughters of Philip (Acts 21:9). God called Deborah a prophetess and a judge, but she saw herself as a *mother* to her people. "I, Deborah arose, that I arose a mother in Israel" (Jud. 5:7). The wayward Jews were her children, and she welcomed them and counseled them.

God revealed to Deborah that Barak ("lightning") was to assemble and lead the Israelite army and draw Sisera's troops into a trap near Mount Tabor; and there the Lord would defeat them. Mount Tabor lies at the juncture of Zebulun, Naphtali, and Issachar, not far from the Kishon River. If Barak would lead the Israelite army toward Mount Tabor, God would draw Sisera and his troops toward the Kishon River, where God would give Barak the victory.

When God wants to glorify Himself through His people, He always has a perfect plan for us to follow. God chose the leader of His army, the place for the battle, and the plan for His army to follow. God also guaranteed the victory. It was like the "good old days" of Joshua again!

3. Act three: a reluctant participant (Jud. 4:8-10)

We aren't told that Barak was a judge, which explains why he got his orders from Deborah, God's appointed leader in the land. Barak was from Naphtali, one of the tribes that would send volunteers to the battlefield (v. 6). Like Moses before him (Ex. 3–4), and Gideon (Jud. 6) and Jeremiah (Jer. 1) after him, Barak hesitated when told what God wanted him to do.

We know that "God's commandments are God's enablements" and that we should obey HIs will in spite of circumstances, feelings, or consequences. But we don't always do it! Was Barak's response an evidence of unbelief or a mark of humility? He didn't accuse God of making a mistake; all he did was ask Deborah to go with him to the battle. Was that because she was a prophetess and he might need a word from the Lord? Or was it to help him enlist more volunteers for the army? The fact that Deborah agreed to accompany Barak suggests that his request wasn't out of God's will, although in granting it, God took the honor from the men and gave it to the women.

Barak enlisted 10,000 men from his own tribe of Naphtali and the neighboring tribe of Zebulun (Jud. 4:6, 10; 5:14, 18). Later, volunteers from the tribes of Benjamin, Ephraim, and Manasseh west (v. 14), and Issachar (v. 15), joined these men, and the army grew to 40,000 men (v. 8). It's possible that the original 10,000 soldiers initiated the campaign that lured Sisera into the trap, and then the other 30,000 joined them for the actual battle and "mopping up" operation. The tribes that were summoned but refused to come were Reuben, Dan, Asher, and Manasseh east (vv. 15-17).

When you consider that weapons were scarce in Israel (5:8;[3] 1 Sam. 13:19-22) and that there was no effective standing army, what Deborah and Barak did was indeed an act of faith. But God had promised to give them victory, and they were depending on His promise (Rom. 10:17).

4. Act four: a victorious confrontation (Jud. 4:11-23)
The Lord is the leading actor in this scene. He not only controlled the enemy army and brought it into the trap, but

He also controlled the weather and used a storm to defeat Sisera's troops.

Sisera is warned (vv. 11-12). Verse 12 suggests that it was Heber and his family who first warned Sisera that the Jews were about to revolt and where the Israelite army was mustering. We met the Kenites in 1:16 and discovered that they were distant relatives of the Jews through Moses. It seems strange that Heber the Kenite would separate himself from his people, who worshiped Jehovah, and be friendly with idolatrous tyrants like Jabin and Sisera (4:17). Perhaps he needed the protection and business of the Canaanites as he carried on his trade as an itinerant metalworker. The Kenites seem to be attached to the tribe of Judah (1:16); but the men of Judah weren't among the volunteers in Barak's army.

It's possible, however, to view Heber from another perspective and see him as a part of God's plan to lure Sisera into the trap. Heber wasn't an ally of Jabin's; he was simply trying to maintain a neutral position in a divided society. But once the Jewish army was in place at Mount Tabor, Heber ran and gave the news to Sisera; and Sisera had no reason to question the report. Sisera began to move his army and fell right into the trap.

Sisera is defeated (vv. 13-16). The Canaanites depended on their 900 iron chariots to give them the advantage they needed as they met the Jewish army (1:19; see Josh. 17:18). What they didn't know was that the Lord would send a fierce rainstorm that would make the Kishon River overflow and turn the battlefield into a sea of mud (Jud. 5:20-22). The water and mud would severely impede the mobility of the Canaanite chariots and horses, and this situation would make it easy for the Israelite soldiers to attack and slaughter the enemy. The trap worked, and the enemy army was wiped out.

Along with the storm from the heavens and the flood from the swollen river, God sent confusion in the minds of the enemy troops. The word translated "routed" (4:15, NKJV) means "confused, thrown into panic." This is what God had done to Pharaoh's charioteers in the Red Sea (Ex. 14:24) and would later do to the Philistines in Samuel's day (1 Sam. 7:10).

One thing that helped to confuse and frighten the Canaanites was the sudden appearance of torrential rain during the traditional dry season. Since Sisera wouldn't have taken his chariots to the fields if he had suspected any kind of bad weather, we can safely assume that this battle was fought during the June-to-September dry season. When you remember that the Canaanite god Baal was the god of storms, you can see how the sudden change of weather could have affected the superstitious Canaanites. Had their own god Baal turned against them? Was the God of Israel stronger than Baal? If so, then the battle was already lost, and the wisest thing the soldiers could do was flee.

Sisera is slain (vv. 17-23). While Barak and his men were pursuing and killing the fleeing Canaanites, some of whom were in chariots and others on foot, the Canaanite captain Sisera was running for his life, probably heading toward Hazor and safety. But weariness got the best of him, and providentially he was near the tents of Heber at the oak of Zaanannim (v. 11). This famous oak was on the border of Naphtali (Josh. 19:33), about six miles east of Mount Tabor.

Since Sisera knew that Heber and his people were friendly toward Jabin, this settlement seemed a good place to stop and rest. When Heber's wife, Jael, came out to meet Sisera and invited him into her tent, the Canaanite captain was sure that he was at last safe. After all, in that culture nobody would dare enter a wife's tent except her husband. Jael gave him milk instead of water and then covered him with a blanket, and he was confident that he had found a dependable ally and could rest in peace.

But Sisera made the mistake of telling Jael to lie if anyone asked whether he was there. Being a wise woman, she concluded that Sisera was fleeing the battlefield, which meant that the Jews had won the battle and the Canaanite grip on the land was broken. If she protected Sisera, she'd be in trouble with the Jews, her own relatives. No doubt somebody was chasing Sisera, and whoever it was wouldn't be satisfied until the captain was dead.

But Sisera had no reason to suspect danger. After all, Heber's clan was friendly to the Canaanites, Jael had shown him hospitality and kindness, and no pursuing Jewish soldier was likely to force his way into a woman's tent. What Sisera didn't know was that God had promised that a woman would take his life (Jud. 4:9).

When Sisera was in a deep sleep, Jael killed him by pounding a tent peg through his head. In the Eastern nomadic tribes, it was the women who put up and took down the tents; so Jael knew how to use a hammer. When Barak arrived on the scene, he discovered that his enemy was dead and that Deborah's prediction had been fulfilled. For a captain to flee from a battle was embarrassing; for him to be killed while fleeing was humiliating; but to be killed by a woman was the most disgraceful thing of all (9:54).

Should we bless or blame Jael for what she did? She invited Sisera into her tent, treated him kindly, and told him not to be afraid; so she was deceitful. The Kenites were at peace with Jabin, so she violated a treaty. She gave Sisera the impression that she would guard the door, so she broke a promise. She killed a defenseless man who was under her protection, so she was a murderess.[4] Yet Deborah sang, "Blessed above women shall Jael the wife of Heber the Kenite be, blessed shall she be above women in the tent" (5:24).

To begin with, let's not read back into the era of the Judges the spiritual standards taught by Jesus and the apostles. Also, let's keep in mind that the Jews had been under terrible bondage because of Jabin and Sisera; and it was God's will that the nation be delivered. Both Jabin and Sisera had been guilty of mistreating the Jews for years; and if the Canaanite army had won the battle, hundreds of Jewish girls would have been captured and raped (v. 30). Jael not only helped deliver the nation of Israel from bondage, but also she helped to protect the women from the most vicious brutality. She wasn't a Semitic "Lady Macbeth" who murdered her guest for her own personal gain. There was a war on, and this courageous woman finally stopped being neutral and took her stand with the people of God.

5. Act five: a glorious celebration (Jud. 5:1-31)

When they wanted to celebrate special occasions, the Jewish people often expressed themselves in song; so the writer shifts from narrative prose to jubilant poetry. Future generations might forget what the history book said, but they were not likely to forget a festive song. (For other examples, see Ex. 15, Deut. 32, 2 Sam. 1:17-27, and Ps. 18.) The personal pronouns in Judges 5:7, 9, and 13 indicate that this was Deborah's victory song; but just as Barak joined her in the battle, so he joined her in the victory celebration.

A poem or song isn't something you can easily outline because it's a spontaneous emotional expression that often defies analysis. Unlike classical English poetry, Hebrew poetry contains recurring themes, expressed in different ways and frequent outbursts of praise and prayer. The following outline is only a suggested approach to this magnificent song of victory.

Praise the Lord, all you people! (vv. 1-12) In verses 1-9, Deborah and Barak praise the Lord for all that He did for His people. He gave unity to the leaders so that Barak could assemble an army (v. 2; and see v. 9). The same God who gave Israel victory in the past would give them victory again (vv. 4-5). Israel had entered into a covenant with the Lord at Mount Sinai, and He would fulfill His promises to His special people. Since conditions were so terrible in the land that something had to be done, God raised up Deborah to be a mother in Israel (vv. 6-9). The enemy took over because the people had turned from Jehovah to worship false gods. Deborah was concerned about the spiritual life of the people as well as their physical and political welfare. Note that this first section (vv. 2-9) begins and ends with "Praise to the Lord" and "Bless ye the Lord."

According to verses 10 and 11, Deborah and Barak summoned the wealthy nobles ("those who ride on white asses") and the common travelers to join the singers at the wells and praise the Lord for what He did to Jabin's army. Now it was safe to walk the roads, gather at the wells, and leisurely talk together. The people could leave the walled cities where they had run for protection and could return to their villages in peace. It was time for all Israel to praise God for His mercies to them.

This praise stanza closes with a call to action (v. 12). God commanded Deborah to wake up and sing and Barak to wake up and attack the enemy. Because of her faith, Deborah could sing before the battle started as well as after the battle ended.

Praise the Lord for the volunteers (vv. 13-18). Deborah was grateful that the people offered themselves willingly in the service of the Lord (vv. 2, 9) and that the nobles did their share in recruiting soldiers from the tribes (v. 13). Six tribes united in sending volunteers. Except for the people in the town of Meroz (v. 23), the men of Naphtali responded, as did the men of Zebulun, Issachar, Benjamin, Ephraim, and Manasseh west (Machir). The phrase in verse 14, "They that handle the pen of the writer" (literally, "the staff of a scribe"), may refer to the recruiting officers who wrote down the names of the soldiers. They were not "summer soldiers" but brave men who were serious about fighting the Lord's battles.

However, there were four tribes that didn't volunteer and do their share of fighting. The tribe of Reuben pondered the call to arms but finally stayed at home. They were probably considering Deuteronomy 20:1-9, Israel's law of warfare, and examining their hearts to see whether they were qualified to go to war. Since Manasseh east (Gilead) was safe on the other side of the Jordan, they also stayed home (Jud. 5:17). Dan and Asher on the coast also elected not to heed the call to battle. In contrast to these shirkers, the tribes of Zebulun and Naphtali are especially praised for risking their lives in the service of the Lord and their country (v. 18).

Keep in mind that during this period in history "every man did that which was right in his own eyes" (21:25). When Joshua was the commander of Israel's armies, *all* the tribes participated; but when Barak summoned the forces, only half of them went to war against Jabin.[5] The people of God today are not unlike the people of Israel when it comes to God's call for service: some immediately volunteer and follow the Lord; some risk their lives; some give the call serious consideration but say no; and others keep to themselves as though the call had never been given.

Praise the Lord for His victory (vv. 19-23). It's one thing to show up for duty and quite something else to go into battle. Sisera had organized an alliance of the Canaanite kings, and their united forces (with 900 chariots) met the Jewish army at Megiddo on the plain of Jezreel.[6] Since it was the dry season of the year, the charioteers expected to annihilate the army of Israel. But God had other plans. He sent a tremendous rainstorm that turned the Kishon River into a raging torrent and the battlefield into a swamp. A raindrop is a very fragile thing; but if you put enough of them together, you can defeat an army! The army of Israel trusted the Lord to give them victory because this is what He had promised (4:6-9).

Deborah and Barak didn't curse the people of Meroz; it was the angel of the Lord who did it. It must have embarrassed Barak to know that a town in his own tribe of Naphtali had refused to send volunteers to assist in this important battle. "Meroz stands for the shirker," said Phillips Brooks in a famous sermon; "for him who is willing to see other people fight the battles of life, while he simply comes in and takes the spoils."[7] Note that their sin wasn't simply failing to assist *Israel;* they failed to help *the Lord!*

Praise the Lord for a courageous woman (vv. 24-31). Deborah's blessing on Jael reminds us of Gabriel's words to Mary (Luke 1:42). Because of Barak's hesitation, Deborah announced that a woman would get the credit for killing the captain of the enemy army (Jud. 4:8-9). The phrase "smote off his head" in verse 26 doesn't mean that she decapitated him with a hammer and a tent peg. The word means "crushed" or "smashed." With one stroke, she sent the tent peg through his temple, shattered his head, and killed him.[8]

The description of Sisera's death in verse 27 gives the impression that he was standing in the tent when Jael struck him and then fell dead at her feet. But he was lying down asleep when he was slain (v. 18). We may have here some Hebrew poetic license, but it's also possible that in the agony of his death Sisera raised himself up from the tent floor and then sank at her feet and expired.

The singer moves from describing Sisera's death to portraying Sisera's mother watching for her son's return (vv. 28-30). What a pathetic picture of hope where there is no hope! How many people today are looking out the window of false assumptions and expecting something to happen that will never happen. Sisera was dead; he would never come home to his mother's love again. His mother and her attendants kept telling themselves and each other that everything was fine, but it wan't.

The closing prayer (v. 31) contrasts the enemies of the Lord—who like Sisera go out in darkness—with the people who love God, who are like the noonday sun.[9] The battle at Megiddo was more than just a conflict between opposing armies. It was a conflict between the forces of darkness and the forces of light. We either love Christ and walk in the light, or we are His enemy and perish in the darkness.

The curtain comes down on our drama, but I predict that the cast will be making curtain calls as long as people read and study the Bible. "For whatever things were written before were written for our learning, that we through the patience and comfort of the Scriptures might have hope" (Rom. 15:4, NKJV).

God's Man in Manasseh

You have a garden, and you work hard all spring and summer to make that garden produce abundantly. But every year, just about the time you're ready to gather in the harvest, your neighbors swoop down and take your produce away from you by force. This goes on year after year, and there's nothing you can do about it.

If you can imagine that scenario, then you'll have some idea of the suffering the Jews experienced every harvest when the Midianites made their annual raids. For seven years, God allowed the Midianites and their allies to ravage "the land of milk and honey," leaving the people in the deepest poverty.

About the time of the eighth Midianite invasion, God called a farmer in Manasseh named Gideon to become the deliverer of His people. Gideon started his career as somewhat of a *coward* (Jud. 6), then became a *conqueror* (7:1–8:21), and ended his career as a *compromiser* (8:22-35). But more space is devoted to Gideon in the Book of Judges (100 verses) than to any other judge;[1] and Gideon is the only judge whose personal struggles with his faith are recorded. Gideon is a great encouragement to people who have a hard time accepting themselves and believing that God can make anything out of them or do anything with them.

But before the Lord could use Gideon in His service, He had to deal with four doubts that plagued him and were obstacles to his faith. These doubts can be expressed in four questions.

1. "Does God really care about us?" (Jud. 6:1-13)

"The Lord has forsaken us!" was Gideon's response to the Lord's message (v. 13, NKJV); and yet the Lord had given Israel proof of His personal concern.

He had chastened them (vv. 1-6). "My son, do not despise the chastening of the Lord, nor detest His correction; for whom the Lord loves He corrects, just as a father the son in whom he delights" (Prov. 3:11-12, NKJV; and see Heb. 12:5-11). Charles Spurgeon said, "The Lord does not permit His children to sin successfully." God is not a "permissive parent" who allows His children to do as they please, for His ultimate purpose is that they might be "conformed to the image of His Son" (Rom. 8:29). The Father wants to be able to look at each member of His spiritual family and say, "This is My beloved child, in whom I am well pleased" (see Matt. 3:17; 12:18; 17:5).

Chastening is evidence of God's hatred for sin and His love for His people. We can't conceive of a holy God wanting anything less than His very best for His children, and the best He can give us is a holy character like that of Jesus Christ. Obedience to the Lord builds character, but sin destroys character; and God cannot sit idly by and watch His children destroy themselves.

Israel had already experienced forty-three years of suffering under the harsh rule of the neighboring nations, but they hadn't yet learned their lesson and turned away from the heathen idols. Unless our suffering leads to repentance, it accomplishes no lasting good; and unless our repentance is evidence of a holy desire to turn from sin, not just escape from pain, repentance is only remorse. Chastening assures us that we are truly God's children, that our Father loves us, and that we can't get away with rebellion.

The Midianites organized a coalition of nations to invade the land (Jud. 6:3), and all that Israel could do was flee to the hills and hide from the enemy. When the Jews returned to their homes, they found only devastation; and they had to face another year without adequate food.

He had rebuked them (vv. 7-10). Previous to this, an angel of the Lord, probably the Son of God, had come to Bochim to reprove Israel for her sins (2:1-5); and now an unnamed prophet came to repeat the message.[2] Often in the Old Testament, when the Lord denounced His people for their disobedience, He reminded them of the wonderful way He had delivered them from Egypt. He also reminded them of His generosity in giving them the land and helping them overcome their enemies. If the Jews were suffering from Gentile bondage, it wasn't God's fault! He had given them everything they needed.

When you read the New Testament epistles, you can't help but notice that the apostles took the same approach when they admonished the believers to whom they wrote. The apostles repeatedly reminded the Christians that God had saved them so that they might live obediently and serve the Lord faithfully. As God's children, they were to walk worthy of their high and heavenly calling (Eph. 4:1) and live like people who were seated with Christ in glory (Col. 3:1ff). The motive for Christian living is not that we might gain something we don't have but that we might live up to what we already have in Christ.

The purpose of chastening is to make God's children willing to listen to God's Word. Often after spanking a child, parents will reassure the child of their love and then gently admonish the child to listen to what they say *and obey it*. God speaks to His children, either through the loving voice of Scripture or the heavy hand of chastening; and if we ignore the first, we must endure the second. One way or another, the Lord is going to get our attention and deal with us.

Now He came down to help them (vv. 11-13). The people were crying out to the Lord for help (6:7), as people usually do when they're in trouble. The Israelites gave no evidence of real repentance, but their affliction moved God's loving heart. "In all their affliction He was afflicted" (Isa. 63:9). "He does not treat us as our sins deserve or repay us according to our iniquities" (Ps. 103:10, NIV). God in His mercy doesn't give us what we do deserve; and in His grace, He gives us what we don't deserve.

When you consider the kind of man Gideon was at this time, you wonder why God selected him; but God often chooses the "weak things of this world" to accomplish great things for His glory (1 Cor. 1:26-29).[3] Gideon's family worshiped Baal (Jud. 6:25-32), although we have no reason to believe that Gideon joined them. When Gideon called himself "the least in my father's house" (v. 15), he may have been suggesting that his family treated him like an outcast because he didn't worship Baal. Gideon wasn't a man of strong faith or courage, and God had to patiently work with him to prepare him for leadership. God is always ready to make us what we ought to be if we're willing to submit to His will (Eph. 2:10; Phil. 2:12-13).

Gideon's negative response to the Lord's words indicates his lack of faith and spiritual perception. Here was Almighty God telling him that He was with him and would make him a conqueror, and Gideon replied by denying everything God said! God would have to spend time with Gideon turning his question marks into exclamation points. Gideon was living by sight, not by faith, and had he remained that way he would never have been named among the heroes of faith in Hebrews 11.

2. "Does God know what He's doing?" (Jud. 6:14-24)

Gideon's first response was to question *God's concern* for His people, but then he questioned *God's wisdom* in choosing him to be the nation's deliverer. The Lord's statements recorded in verses 12 and 14 should have given Gideon all the assurance he needed, but he wouldn't believe God's Word. In this, he was like Moses (Ex. 3:7-12), whose story Gideon surely knew since he was acquainted with Hebrew history (Jud. 6:13).

It has often been said that "God's commandments are God's enablements." Once God has called and commissioned us, all we have to do is obey Him by faith, and He will do the rest. God cannot lie and God never fails. Faith means obeying God in spite of what we see, how we feel, or what the consequences might be. Our modern "practical" world laughs at faith without realizing that people live by faith all day long. "If there was no faith, there would be no living in this world," wrote humorist John Billings nearly a century ago. "We couldn't even eat hash with safety."

Gideon's statement about the poverty of his family is a bit perplexing in the light of the fact that he had ten servants who assisted him (v. 27). It may be that the clan of Abiezer, to which Gideon's family belonged, was not an important clan in Manasseh; or perhaps Gideon's statement was simply the standard way to respond to a compliment, as when people used to sign their letters "Your Obedient Servant." In any event, Gideon seemed to think that God could *do* nothing because he and his family *were* nothing.

Once God has revealed His will to us, we must never question His wisdom or argue with His plans. "Who has known the mind of the Lord? Or who has been His counsel-or?" (Rom. 11:34, NIV; see Isa. 40:13 and 1 Cor. 2:16) "Can you search out the deep things of God? Can you find out the limits of the Almighty?" (Job 11:7, NKJV) A.W. Tozer wrote, "All God's acts are done in perfect wisdom, first for His own glory, and then for the highest good of the greatest number for the longest time."[4] That being true, who are we to ques-tion Him?

When you review God's gracious promises to Gideon, you wonder why this young man wavered in his faith. God prom-ised to be with him. God called him a "mighty man of valor" and promised that he would save Israel from the Midianites and smite them "as one man." God's Word is "the word of faith" (Rom. 10:8), and "faith comes by hearing, and hearing by the Word of God" (Rom. 10:17). But Gideon didn't receive that Word and needed assurance beyond the character of Almighty God.

Gideon asked for a sign to assure him that it was really the Lord who was speaking to him (1 Cor. 1:22), and the Lord was gracious to accommodate Himself to Gideon's unbelief. Gideon prepared a sacrifice, which was a costly thing to do at a time when food was scarce. An ephah of flour was about a half a bushel, enough to make bread for a family for several days. It probably took him an hour to dress the meat and prepare the unleavened cakes, but God waited for him to return and then consumed the offering by bringing fire from the rock.

The sudden appearance of the fire and disappearance of the visitor convinced Gideon that indeed he had seen God and spoken to Him, and this frightened him even more. Since the Jews believed it was fatal for sinful man to look upon God, Gideon was sure he would die. The human heart is indeed deceitful: Gideon asked to see a sign, and after seeing it, he was sure that the God who gave him the sign would now kill him! There is always "joy and peace in believing" (Rom. 15:13), but unbelief brings fear and worry.

God had to give Gideon a message of peace to prepare him for fighting a war. Unless we're at peace with God, we can't face the enemy with confidence and fight the Lord's battles. It was customary for the Jews to identify special events and places by putting up monuments,[5] so Gideon built an altar and called it "The Lord is peace." The Hebrew word for "peace" (shalom) means much more than a cessation of hostilities but carries with it the ideas of well-being, health, and prosperity. Gideon now believed the Lord was able to use him, not because of who he was but because of who God was.

Whenever God calls us to a task that we think is beyond us, we must be careful to look to God and not to ourselves. "Is anything too hard for the Lord?" God asked Abraham (Gen. 18:14); and the answer comes, "For with God nothing shall be impossible" (Luke 1:37). Job discovered that God could do everything (Job 42:2), and Jeremiah admitted that there was nothing too hard for God (Jer. 32:17). Jesus told His disciples, "With God all things are possible" (Matt. 19:26); and Paul testified, "I can do all things through Christ who strengthens me" (Phil. 4:13, NKJV).

3. "Will God take care of me?" (Jud. 6:25-32)

What kind of a day did Gideon have after his dramatic meeting with the Lord? Remember, he belonged to a family that worshiped Baal; and if he challenged the Midianites in the name of the Lord, it meant defying his father, his family, his neighbors, and the multitudes of people in Israel who were worshiping Baal. My guess is that Gideon had his emotional ups and downs that day, rejoicing that God was planning to deliver Israel, but trembling at the thought of being named the leader of the army.

Knowing that Gideon was still afraid, God assigned him a

task right at home to show him that He would see him through. After all, if we don't practice our faith at home, how can we practice it sincerely anyplace else? Gideon had to take his stand in his own village before he dared to face the enemy on the battlefield.

Before God gives His servants great victories in public, He sometimes prepares them by giving them smaller victories at home. Before David killed the giant Goliath in the sight of two armies, he learned to trust God by killing a lion and a bear in the field where nobody saw it but God (1 Sam. 17:32-37). When we prove that we're faithful with a few things, God will trust us with greater things (Matt. 25:21).

The assignment wasn't an easy one. God told him to destroy the altar dedicated to Baal, build an altar to the Lord, and sacrifice one of his father's valuable bullocks, using the wood of the Asherah pole for fuel. Jewish altars were made of uncut stones and were simple, but Baal's altars were elaborate and next to them was a wooden pillar ("grove," Jud. 6:26; "Asherah pole," NIV) dedicated to the goddess Asherah, whose worship involved unspeakably vile practices. Since altars to Baal were built on high places, it would have been difficult to obey God's orders without attracting attention.

Gideon had every right to destroy Baal worship because this is what God had commanded in His Law (Ex. 34:12-13; Deut. 7:5). For that matter, he had the right to stone everybody who was involved in Baal worship (Deut. 13), but God didn't include that in His instructions.

Gideon decided to obey the Lord at night when the village was asleep. This showed his fear (Jud. 6:27); he wasn't sure God could or would see him through. "Why are you so fearful? How is it that you have no faith?" (Mark 4:40, NKJV) "Behold, God is my salvation, I will trust and not be afraid" (Isa. 12:2, NKJV). After all the encouragements God had given him, Gideon's faith should have been strong; but before we judge him, we'd better look at ourselves and see how much *we* trust the Lord.

It's worth noting that true believers can't build an altar to the Lord unless first they tear down the altars they've built to the false gods they worship. Our God is a jealous God (Ex. 20:5) and will not share His glory or our love with another. Gideon had privately built his own altar to the Lord (Jud. 6:24), but now he had to take his public stand; and he had to do it without compromise. Before he could declare war on Midian, he had to declare war on Baal.

When ten other men are involved, it's not easy to keep your plans a secret; so it wasn't long before the whole town knew that Gideon was the one who had destroyed his father's idols. The men of the city considered this a capital offense and wanted to kill Gideon. (According to God's law, it was the idol-worshipers who should have been slain! See Deut. 13:6-9.) Gideon was no doubt wondering what would happen to him, but God proved Himself well able to handle the situation.

Joash, Gideon's father, had every reason to be angry with his son. Gideon had smashed his father's altar to Baal and replaced it with an altar to Jehovah. He had sacrificed his father's prize bull to the Lord and had used the sacred Asherah pole for fuel. (See Isa. 44:13-20.) But God so worked in Joash's heart that he defended Gideon before the town mob and even insulted Baal! "What kind of a god is Baal that he can't even defend himself?" asked Joash. (Elijah would take a similar approach years later. See 1 Kings 18:27.) "What kind of a god is Baal that he can't even plead his own cause?" Joash asked. Because of this, the men of the town gave Gideon the nickname "Jerubbaal," which means "let Baal contend" or "Baal's antagonist."[6]

Often the unbelieving world gives demeaning nicknames to faithful servants of God. D.L. Moody was known as "Crazy

Moody" when he was building his famous Sunday School in Chicago, but nobody would call him that today; and Charles Spurgeon was frequently lampooned and caricatured in the British press. If we are given nicknames because we honor the name of Jesus, then let's wear them like medals and keep on glorifying Him!

Gideon learned a valuable lesson that day: If he obeyed the Lord, even with fear in his heart, the Lord would protect him and receive the glory. Gideon needed to remember this as he mustered his army and prepared to attack the enemy.

4. "Does God keep His promises?" (Jud. 6:33-40)

The Midianites and their allies made their annual invasion about that time as more than 135,000 men (8:10; 7:12) moved into the Valley of Jezreel. It was time for Gideon to act, and the Spirit of God gave him the wisdom and power that he needed. (See Jud. 3:10; 11:29; 13:25; 14:6, 19; 15:14.) As we seek to do God's will, His Word to us is always, "Not by might, nor by power, but by My spirit" (Zech. 4:6).

When a group of British pastors was discussing the advisability of inviting evangelist D.L. Moody to their city for a crusade, one man asked, "Why must it be Moody? Does D.L. Moody have a monopoly on the Holy Spirit?" Quietly one of the other pastors replied, "No, but it's evident that the Holy Spirit has a monopoly on D.L. Moody."

Gideon blew the trumpet first in his own hometown, and the men of Abiezer rallied behind him. Gideon's reformation in the town had actually accomplished something! Then he sent messengers throughout his own tribe of Manasseh as well as the neighboring tribes of Asher, Zebulun, and Naphtali. These four tribes were near the Valley of Jezreel, and therefore the invading army affected them most. Thus at Gideon's call, 32,000 men responded.

But what chance did 32,000 men have against an army of

135,000 men plus numberless camels? (Jud. 7:12) This is the first mention in the Bible of camels being used in warfare, and certainly they would have given their riders speed and mobility on the battlefield. The Jews were outnumbered and would certainly be outmaneuvered, except for one thing: Jehovah God was on their side, and He had promised them victory.

Nevertheless, Gideon doubted God's promise. Did God really want *him* to lead the Jewish army? What did he know about warfare? After all, he was only an ordinary farmer; and there were others in the tribes who could do a much better job. So, before he led the attack, he asked God to give him two more signs.

The phrase "putting out the fleece" is a familiar one in religious circles. It means asking God to guide us in a decision by fulfilling some condition that we lay down. In my pastoral ministry, I've met all kinds of people who have gotten themselves into trouble by "putting out the fleece." If they received a phone call at a certain hour from a certain person, God was telling them to do this; or if the weather changed at a certain time, God was telling them to do something else.

"Putting out the fleece" is not a biblical method for determining the will of God. Rather, it's an approach used by people like Gideon who lack the faith to trust God to do what He said He would do. Twice Gideon reminded God of what He had said (6:36-37), and twice Gideon asked God to reaffirm His promises with a miracle. The fact that God stooped to Gideon's weakness only proves that He's a gracious God who understands how we're made (Ps. 103:14).[7] Who are we to tell God what conditions He must meet, especially when He has already spoken to us in His Word? "Putting out the fleece" is not only an evidence of our unbelief, but it's also an evidence of our pride. God has to do what I tell Him to do

before I'll do what He tells me to do!

Gideon spent two days playing the fleece game with God at the threshing floor. The first night, he asked God to make the fleece wet but keep the ground dry (in this incident the Bible uses "floor" and "ground" interchangeably) and God did it. The second night, the test was much harder; for he wanted the threshing floor to be wet but the fleece dry. The ground of a threshing floor is ordinarily very hard and normally would not be greatly affected by the dew. But the next morning, Gideon found dry fleece but wet ground.

There was nothing for Gideon to do but to confront the enemy and trust God for the victory. "And this is the victory that has overcome the world—our faith" (1 John 5:4, NKJV).

FIVE

Faith Is the Victory

I don't recall too many chapel messages from my years as a seminary student, but Vance Havner gave a message that has stayed with me and often encouraged me. Speaking from Hebrews 11, he told us that because Moses was a man of faith, he was able to "see the invisible, choose the imperishable, and do the impossible." I needed that message then and I still need it today.

What was true for Moses centuries ago can be true for God's people today, but men and women of faith seem to be in short supply. Whatever our churches may be known for today, they're not especially known for glorifying God by great exploits of faith. "The church used to be known for its good deeds," said one wit, "but today it's better known for its bad mortgages."

"For whatever is born of God overcomes the world. And this is the victory that has overcome the world—our faith" (1 John 5:4, NKJV). Christians are either overcome because of their unbelief or overcomers because of their faith. And remember, faith doesn't depend on how we feel, what we see, or what may happen. The Quaker poet John Greenleaf Whittier put it this way in "My Soul and I":

Nothing before, nothing behind;
The steps of faith
Fall on the seeming void, and find
The rock beneath.

That rock is the Word of God.

The familiar and exciting account of Gideon's wonderful victory over the Midianites is really a story of faith in action, and it reveals to us three important principles about faith. If we're to be overcomers, and not be overcome, we need to understand and apply these principles.

1. God tests our faith (Jud. 7:1-8)

A faith that can't be tested can't be trusted. Too often, what people think is faith is really only a "warm fuzzy feeling" about faith or perhaps just "faith in faith." I recall being in a board meeting of an international ministry when one of the board members said enthusiastically, "We're simply going to have to step out by faith!" Quietly another board member asked, "Whose faith?" That question made all of us search our hearts.

J.G. Stipe said that faith is like a toothbrush: Everybody should have one and use it regularly, but it isn't safe to use somebody else's. We can sing loudly about the "Faith of Our Fathers," but we can't exercise the faith of our fathers. We can follow men and women of faith and share in their exploits, but we can't succeed in our own personal lives by depending on somebody else's faith.

God tests our faith for at least two reasons: first, to show us whether our faith is real or counterfeit, and second, to strengthen our faith for the tasks He's set before us. I've noticed in my own life and ministry that God has often put us through the valley of testing before allowing us to reach the mountain peak of victory. Spurgeon was right when he said that the promises of God shine brightest in the furnace of affliction, and it is in claiming those promises that we gain the victory.

The first sifting (vv. 1-3). God tested Gideon's faith by sifting his army of 32,000 volunteers until only 300 men were left. If Gideon's faith had been in the size of his army, then his faith would have been very weak by the time God was through with them! Less than 1 percent of the original 32,000 ended up following Gideon to the battlefield. The words of Winston Churchill concerning the RAF in World War II certainly applies to Gideon's 300: "Never in the field of human conflict was so much owed to so many by so few."

God told Gideon why He was decreasing the size of the army: He didn't want the soldiers to boast that they had won the victory over the Midianites. Victories won because of faith bring glory to God because nobody can explain how they happened. "If you can explain what's going on in your ministry," Dr. Bob Cook used to remind us, "then God didn't do it." When I was serving in Youth for Christ, I often heard our leaders pray, "Lord, keep Youth for Christ on a miracle basis." That meant living by faith.

Too often, we're like King Uzziah who was "marvelously helped, till he was strong. But when he was strong, his heart was lifted up to his destruction" (2 Chron. 26:15-16). People who live by faith know their own weakness more and more as they depend on God's strength. "For when I am weak, then am I strong" (2 Cor. 12:10).

In telling the fearful soldiers to return home, Gideon was simply obeying the law Moses originally gave: "What man is there who is fearful and fainthearted? Let him go and return to his house, lest the heart of his brethren faint like his heart" (Deut. 20:8, NKJV). "The fearful and trembling man God cannot use," said G. Campbell Morgan. "The trouble today is that the fearful and trembling man insists upon re-

maining in the army. A decrease that
Church of men who fear and tremble is
and a glorious gain."[1]

Pride after the battle robs God of glory, and
battle robs God's soldiers of courage and powe   s a
way of spreading, and one timid soldier can do m   amage
than a whole company of enemy soldiers. Fear and faith can't
live together very long in the same heart. Either fear will
conquer faith and we'll quit, or faith will conquer fear and
we'll triumph. John Wesley may have been thinking of Gideon's army when he said, "Give me a hundred men who fear
nothing but sin and love nothing but God, and I will shake the
gates of hell!"[2]

The second sifting (vv. 4-8). God put Gideon's surviving
10,000 men through a second test by asking them all to take
a drink down at the river. *We never know when God is testing
us in some ordinary experience of life.* I heard about one leading minister who always took a drive with a prospective pastoral staff member *in the other man's car,* just to see if the car
was neat and if the man drove carefully. Whether or not
neatness and careful driving habits are always a guarantee of
ministerial success is debatable, but the lesson is worth considering. More than one prospective employee has ruined his
or her chances for a job while having lunch with the boss, not
realizing they were being evaluated. "Make every occasion a
great occasion, for you can never tell when somebody may be
taking your measure for a larger place." That was said by a
man named Marsden; and I've had the quotation, now yellow
with age, under the glass on my desk for many years. Pon-
dering it from time to time has done me good.

What significance was there in the two different ways the
men drank from the river? Since the Scriptures don't tell us,
we'd be wise not to read into the text some weighty spiritual
lesson that God never put there. Most expositors say the

_n who bowed down to drink were making themselves vulnerable to the enemy, while the 300 who lapped water from their hands stayed alert. But the enemy was four miles away (v. 1), waiting to see what the Jews would do; and Gideon wouldn't have led his men into a dangerous situation like that. One well-known preacher claims that the 300 men drank as they did so they could keep their eyes on Gideon, but the text doesn't say that either.

My assumption is that God chose this method of sifting the army because it was simple, unassuming (no soldier knew he was being tested), and easy to apply. We shouldn't think that all 10,000 drank at one time, because that would have stretched the army out along the water for a couple of miles. Since the men undoubtedly came to the water by groups, Gideon was able to watch them and identify the 300. It wasn't until after the event that the men discovered they had been tested.

"There is no restraint to the Lord to save by many or by few" (1 Sam. 14:6). Some churches today are mesmerized by statistics and think they're strong because they're big and wealthy, but numbers are no guarantee of God's blessing. Moses assured the Jews that if they would obey the Lord, one soldier could chase a thousand and two would "put ten thousand to flight" (Deut. 32:30). All Gideon needed was 27 soldiers to defeat the whole Midianite army of 135,000 men (Jud. 8:10), but God gave him 300.

It is clear from 7:14 that the Midianites knew who Gideon was, and no doubt they were watching what he was doing. I've often wondered what the enemy spies thought when they saw the Jewish army seemingly fall apart. Did it make the Midianites overconfident and therefore less careful? Or did their leaders become even more alert, wondering whether Gideon was setting them up for a tricky piece of strategy?

God graciously gave Gideon one more promise of victory:

"By the 300 men that lapped will I save you" (v. 7). By claiming this promise and obeying the Lord's directions, Gideon defeated the enemy and brought peace to the land for forty years (8:28).

The soldiers who departed left some of their equipment with the 300 men thus each man could have a torch, a trumpet, and a jar—strange weapons indeed for fighting a war.

2. God encourages our faith (Jud. 7:9-15a)

The Lord wanted Gideon and his 300 men to attack the camp of Midian that night, but first He had to deal with the fear that still persisted in Gideon's heart. God had already told Gideon three times that He would give Israel victory (6:14, 16; 7:7), and He had reassured him by giving him three special signs: fire from the rock (6:19-21), the wet fleece (6:36-38), and the dry fleece (6:39-40). After all this divine help, Gideon should have been strong in his faith, but such was not the case.

How grateful we should be that God understands us and doesn't condemn us because we have doubts and fears! He keeps giving us wisdom and doesn't scold us when we keep asking (James 1:5). Our great High Priest in heaven sympathizes with our weaknesses (Heb. 4:14-16) and keeps giving us more grace (James 4:6). God remembers that we're only dust (Ps. 103:14) and flesh (78:39).

God encouraged Gideon's faith in two ways.

God gave Gideon another promise (v. 9). The Lord told Gideon for the fourth time that He had delivered the Midianite host into his hand. (Note the tense of the verb, and see Josh. 6:2.) Although the battle must be fought, Israel had already won! The 300 men could attack the enemy host confident that Israel was the victor.

Some people have the idea that confident, courageous faith is a kind of religious arrogance, but just the opposite is true.

Christians who believe God's promises and see Him do great things are humbled to know that the God of the universe cares about them and is on their side. They claim no merit in their faith or honor from their victories. All the glory goes to the Lord because He did it all! It's the unbelieving child of God who grieves the Lord and makes Him a liar (1 John 5:10).

Hope and love are important Christian virtues, but the Holy Spirit devoted an entire chapter in the New Testament — Hebrews 11 — to the victories of *faith* won by ordinary people who dared to believe God and act upon His promises. It may be a cliché to some people, but the old formula is still true: "God says it — I believe — it that settles it!"

God gave Gideon another sign (vv. 10-14). It took courage for Gideon and his servant to move into enemy territory and get close enough to the Midianite camp to overhear the conversation of two soldiers. God had given one of the soldiers a dream, and that dream told Gideon that God would deliver the Midianites into his hand. The Lord had already told Gideon this fact, but now Gideon heard it from the lips of the enemy!

In the biblical record, you often find God communicating His truth through dreams. Among the believers He spoke to through dreams are Jacob (Gen. 28, 31), Joseph (Gen. 37), Solomon (1 Kings 3), Daniel (Dan. 7), and Joseph, the husband of Mary (Matt. 1:20-21; 2:13-22). But He also spoke to unbelievers this way, including Abimelech (Gen. 20), Nebuchadnezzar (Dan. 2, 4), Joseph's fellow prisoners (Gen. 40), Pharaoh (Gen. 41), and Pilate's wife (Matt. 27:19). However, we must not conclude from these examples that this is the Lord's normal method of communicating with people or that we should seek His guidance in our dreams today. Dreams can be deceptive (Jer. 23:32; Zech. 10:2), and apart from divine instruction we can't know the correct interpretation.

The best way to get God's guidance is through the Word of God, prayer, and sensitivity to the Spirit as we watch circumstances.

Since barley was a grain used primarily by poor people, the barley-cake image of Gideon and his army spoke of their weakness and humiliation. The picture is that of a stale hard cake that could roll like a wheel, not a complimentary comparison at all! The man who interpreted the dream had no idea that he was speaking God's truth and encouraging God's servant. Gideon didn't mind being compared to a loaf of stale bread, for now he knew for sure that Israel would defeat the Midianites and deliver the land from bondage.

It's significant that Gideon paused to worship the Lord before he did anything else. He was so overwhelmed by the Lord's goodness and mercy that he fell on his face in submission and gratitude. Joshua did the same thing before taking the city of Jericho (Josh. 5:13-15), and it's a good practice for us to follow today. Before we can be successful warriors, we must first become sincere worshipers.

3. God honors our faith (Jud. 7:15b-25)

"But without faith it is impossible to please Him, for he who comes to God must believe that He is, and that He is a rewarder of those who diligently seek Him" (Heb. 11:6, NKJV). Faith means more than simply trusting God; it also means *seeking* God and wanting to *please* Him. We don't trust God just to get Him to do things for us. We trust Him because it brings joy to His heart when His children rely on Him, seek Him, and please Him.

How did God reward Gideon's faith?

God gave him wisdom to prepare the army (7:15b-18). Gideon was a new man when he and his servant returned to the Israelite camp. His fears and doubts were gone as he mobilized his small army and infused courage into their hearts by what he said and did. "The Lord has delivered the camp of Midian into your hand," he announced to the men (v. 15, NKJV). As Vance Havner said, faith sees the invisible (victory in a battle not yet fought) and does the impossible (wins the battle with few men and peculiar weapons).

Gideon's plan was simple but effective. He gave each of his men a trumpet to blow, a jar to break, and a torch to burn. They would encircle the enemy camp, the torches inside the jars and their trumpets in their hands. The trumpets were rams' horns (the *shofar)* such as Joshua used at Jericho, and perhaps this connection with that great victory helped encourage Gideon and his men as they faced the battle. At Gideon's signal, the men would blow the trumpets, break the pitchers, reveal the lights, and then shout, "The sword of the Lord and of Gideon!" God would do the rest.

Gideon was the example for them to follow. "Watch me. . . . Follow my lead. . . . Do exactly as I do" (v. 17, NIV). Gideon had come a long way since the day God had found him hiding in the winepress! No longer do we hear him asking "If—why—where?" (6:13) No longer does he seek for a sign. Instead, he confidently gave orders to his men, knowing that the Lord would give them the victory.

It has been well said that the Good News of the Gospel is we don't have to stay the way we are. Through faith in Jesus Christ, anybody can be changed. "Therefore, if anyone is in Christ, he is a new creation; old things have passed away; behold, all things have become new" (2 Cor. 5:17, NKJV). Jesus said to Andrew's brother, "You are Simon ["a hearer"]. . . . You shall be called Cephas ["a stone"]" (John 1:42, NKJV). "You are—you shall be!" That's good news for anybody who wants a new start in life. God can take a weak piece of clay like Simon and make a rock out of him! God can take a doubter like Gideon and make a general out of him!

God gave him courage to lead the army (vv. 19-22). Gideon

led his small army from the Spring of Harod ("trembling") to the Valley of Jezreel, where they all took their places around the camp. At Gideon's signal, they all blew their rams' horns, broke the jars, and shouted, "The sword of the Lord and of Gideon!" Finding themselves surrounded by sudden light and loud noises, the Midianites assumed that they were being attacked by a large army, and the result was panic. The Lord intervened and put a spirit of confusion in the camp, and the Midianites began to kill each other. Then they realized that the safest thing to do was flee. Thus they took off on the caravan route to the southeast with the Israelite army pursuing.

God gave him opportunity to enlarge the army (vv. 23-25). It was obvious that 300 men couldn't pursue thousands of enemy soldiers, so Gideon sent out a call for more volunteers. I'm sure that many of the men from the original army of 32,000 responded to Gideon's call, and even the proud tribe of Ephraim came to his aid. To them was given the honor of capturing and slaying Oreb ("raven") and Zeeb ("wolf"), the two princes of Midian. The story of Gideon began with a man hiding in a winepress (6:11), but it ended with the enemy prince being slain at a winepress.

Gideon's great victory over the Midianites became a landmark event in the history of Israel, not unlike the Battle of Waterloo for Great Britain, for it reminded the Jews of God's power to deliver them from their enemies. The day of Midian was a great day that Israel would never forget (Ps. 83:11; Isa. 9:4; 10:26).

The church today can also learn from this event and be encouraged by it. God doesn't need large numbers to accomplish His purposes, nor does He need especially gifted leaders. Gideon and his 300 men were available for God to use, and He enabled them to conquer the enemy and bring peace to the land. When the church starts to depend on "bigness"—big buildings, big crowds, big budgets—then faith becomes misplaced, and God can't give His blessing. When leaders depend on their education, skill, and experience rather than in God, then God abandons them and looks for a Gideon.

The important thing is for us to be available for God to use just as He sees fit. We may not fully understand His plans, but we can fully trust His promises; and it's faith in Him that gives the victory.

Win the War, Lose the Victory

Be careful where you travel for business or vacation. You might pick a place that's dangerous.

According to an article in the June 25, 1993 issue of *Pulse*, there are fifty-six nations that have serious problems with land mines. Angola has 20 million mines waiting to maim or kill, Afghanistan 10 million, and Cambodia 4½ million; and the expense of removing them is more than these nations can handle. The wars may be over, but the dangers haven't vanished.

The saintly Scottish Presbyterian pastor Andrew Bonar wasn't thinking particularly about land mines when he said it, but what he said is good counsel for all of us: "Let us be as watchful after the victory as before the battle." That was the counsel Gideon needed after he'd routed the Midianites, because his problems still weren't over. He discovered some "mines" that were ready to explode.

Thus far in our study of Gideon's life, we've seen his responses to the Lord's call to defeat the enemy. At first Gideon was full of questions and doubts; but then he grew in his faith, believed God's promises, and led his army to victory. In Judges 8, the account focuses on Gideon's responses to various people *after he had won the battle;* and it tells us how he handled some difficult situations.

The chronology in chapter 8 seems to be as follows: Gideon's pursuit of the two kings (vv. 4-12); his disciplining of the defiant Jews on his journey home (vv. 13-17); the protest of the Ephraimites after he arrived home (vv. 1-3); the slaying of the kings (vv. 18-21); and Gideon's "retirement" (vv. 22-35). Each of these events presented a new challenge to Gideon, and he responded differently to each one.

1. A soft answer for his critics (Jud. 8:1-3)

Why this paragraph is placed here is somewhat of a puzzle. It's not likely that the men of Ephraim would complain to Gideon while they were capturing Oreb and Zeeb (7:24-25) and while he was pursuing Zebah and Zalmunna (8:12). Fighting the enemy would have consumed all their energy and attention, and Gideon's reply in verse 3 indicates that the men of Ephraim had already captured and killed Oreb and Zeeb. Perhaps a delegation from the tribe waited on Gideon when the spoils of war were being distributed after he returned home, and that's when they complained.

Knowing that they were a large and important tribe, second only to Judah, the Ephraimites were a proud people. Gideon was from Manasseh, the "brother" tribe to Ephraim,[1] and Ephraim was insulted because he didn't call them to the battle. But why would such an important tribe want to follow a farmer into battle? They had assisted Ehud (3:26-29) and Deborah and Barak (5:13-14), but that was no guarantee they would help Gideon.

When you reflect on the way the attack on Midian was handled, it was wisdom on Gideon's part that he hadn't called for volunteers from Ephraim. This proud tribe would have been incensed if Gideon had told the frightened men to go home, and their volunteers would not have tolerated his thinning out the ranks to only 300 soldiers! If Gideon had called them and then sent most of them back, they would have created a far worse problem *before* the battle than they did afterward. Ephraim was on hand to help in the "mopping up" operations, and that's what really counted.

Ephraim, however, missed out on acquiring some valuable spoils of war from over 100,000 soldiers, and this may have been what irritated them. (Usually when people criticize something you've done, there's a personal reason behind their criticism; and you may never find out what the real reason was.) Since David's unselfish law governing the dividing of the spoils of war hadn't been established yet (1 Sam. 30:21-25), those who didn't participate in the battle didn't share in the loot. When the men of Ephraim should have been thanking Gideon for delivering the nation, they were criticizing him and adding to his burdens.

As a victorious general, a national hero, and the people's first choice for king, Gideon might have used his authority and popularity to put the tribe of Ephraim in its place, but he chose to use a better approach. "A soft answer turns away wrath, but a harsh word stirs up anger" (Prov. 15:1, NKJV). Perhaps Gideon's immediate feelings weren't that cordial, but he controlled himself and treated his brothers with kindness. "He who is slow to anger is better than the mighty, and he who rules his spirit than he who takes a city" (16:32, NKJV). Gideon proved that he could control not only an army, but also control his temper and tongue.

It's sad when brothers declare war on each other after they've stood together to defeat the enemy. "Behold, how good and how pleasant it is for brethren to dwell together in unity!" (Ps. 133:1) It didn't cost Gideon much to swallow his pride and compliment the men of Ephraim. He told them that their capturing Oreb and Zeeb was a greater feat than anything the men had done from his hometown of Abiezer. Peace was restored and Gideon returned to the more important tasks at hand.[2]

In *Poor Richard's Almanack* (1734), Benjamin Franklin wrote:

Take this remark from Richard, poor and lame,
Whate'er's begun in anger ends in shame.

And King Solomon wrote, "The beginning of strife is like releasing water; therefore stop contention before a quarrel starts" (Prov. 17:14, NKJV).

2. A stern warning for the skeptics (Jud. 8:4-17)

Gideon and his men were pursuing two of the Midianite kings, Zebah and Zalmunna, knowing that if they captured and killed them, the enemy's power would be crippled and eventually broken. The army crossed over the Jordan to Succoth in Gad, hoping to find some nourishment; but the men of Succoth wouldn't help their own brothers. The two and a half tribes that occupied the land east of the Jordan didn't feel as close to the other tribes as they should have, and Gad had sent no soldiers to help either Deborah and Barak (5:17) or Gideon. While others were risking their lives, the people of Gad were doing nothing.

The Ammonites and Moabites, relatives of the Jews through Lot, failed to help Israel with food; and God declared war on them (Deut. 23:3-6). Hospitality is one of the basic laws of the East, and custom demands that the people meet the needs of strangers as well as relatives. Hospitality was also an important ministry in the early church, for there were no hotels where guests might stay; and in times of persecution, many visitors were fleeing. (See Rom. 12:13; 1 Tim. 5:10; Heb. 13:2; 1 Peter 4:9.) Indeed, helping a hungry brother is an opportunity to help the Lord Jesus (Matt. 25:34-40).

The men of Succoth were skeptical of Gideon's ability to defeat the fleeing Midianite army and capture the two kings. If Succoth helped Gideon and Gideon failed, then the Midianites would visit Succoth and retaliate. The men of Succoth didn't think feeding a hungry brother was an opportunity to show love but was a risk they didn't want to take, and they were rather impudent in the way they spoke to Gideon. Since Gideon received the same response from the men at Peniel (Penuel), he warned both cities that he would return and discipline them.

God gave Gideon and his men victory over the fleeing Midianite hosts and enabled him to capture the two enemy kings. Triumphantly he retraced his steps and kept his promise to the men of Succoth and Peniel. Providentially, he found a young man who was able to give him the names of the seventy-seven leaders in Succoth who had refused to help him and his army. He showed them the two kings whom the elders had said Gideon would never capture, and then he chastised them, apparently by beating them with thorny branches.[3] He then went to Peniel and wrecked their tower, killing the men who had opposed him.

Why didn't Gideon show to the people of Succoth and Peniel the same kindness that he showed to the Ephraimites and simply forgive them their offenses? For one thing, their offenses were not alike. The pride of Ephraim was nothing compared to the rebellion of Succoth and Peniel. Ephraim was protecting their tribal pride, a sin but not a costly one; but Succoth and Peniel were rebelling against God's chosen leader *and assisting the enemy at the same time.* Theirs was the sin of hardness of heart toward their brethren and treason against the God of heaven. Of what good was it for Gideon and his men to risk their lives to deliver Israel if they had traitors right in their own nation?

Leaders must have discernment or they will make wrong

decisions as they deal with different situations. Personal insults are one thing, but rebellion against the Lord and His people is quite something else.

3. A solemn question for his enemies (Jud. 8:18-21)

When Gideon arrived back home at Ophrah, leading Zebah and Zalmunna captive, the procession must have been as exciting as a ticker-tape parade. Gideon was a true hero. With only 300 men, he had routed the enemy camp and then pursued the fleeing soldiers across the Jordan and as far south as Karkor. He had brought his royal prisoners back, plus whatever spoils the men had gathered along the way.

Gideon had a personal matter to settle with these two kings because they had been guilty of killing his brothers at Tabor. The text doesn't tell us when this wicked act took place, but it must have occurred during one of the previous annual Midianite raids. How Gideon's brothers became involved and why they were killed isn't explained to us, but the suggestion is that the act was a unconscionable one.

According to Mosaic Law, the family was to avenge crimes like this by killing those responsible for the murder. There was no police system in the land, and each family was expected to track down and punish those who had murdered their relatives, provided the culprit was guilty (see Num. 35:9-34). In the case of Zebah and Zalmunna, the culprits were not only murderers but also enemies of Israel.

The two kings were shrewd in the way they answered Gideon, flattering him by comparing him and his brothers to princes. Someone has said that flattery is a good thing to taste but a bad thing to swallow, and Gideon didn't swallow it! How could he spare these two evil men who had taken taken food from the mouths of Jewish women and children and had brutally killed Jewish men?

In those days, how a soldier died was important to his

reputation. Abimelech didn't want to die at the hand of a woman (9:53-54), and King Saul didn't want to fall into the hands of the Philistines (1 Sam. 31:1-6). For a child to kill a king would be the ultimate in humiliation thus Gideon told his young son Jether to execute the two criminals. By doing so, Jether would not only uphold the law of the land and humiliate the two kings, but he would also bring honor to himself. For the rest of his life, he would be known as the boy who executed Zebah and Zalmunna.

But the lad wasn't ready for either the responsibility or the honor. Even when people are guilty, enforcing justice in the land is a serious thing and must not be put into the hands of children. Because of his fear, Jether hesitated in avenging the murders of his uncles; so the two kings told Gideon to do it.

There seems to be a bit of sarcasm in their words, which may be paraphrased, *"You* kill us, Gideon. Let's see what kind of a man *you* are—or are you also just a child?" Zebah and Zalmunna didn't want the inexperienced Jether to execute them because he would have muddled the whole thing and made their deaths much more painful. The kings deliberately aroused Gideon's anger, knowing that he was a good swordsman and would dispatch them quickly, and that's exactly what he did.

4. A puzzling reply for his friends (Jud. 8:22-32)

The narrative focuses on two requests, one from the people to Gideon and the other from Gideon to the people.

The people request a king (vv. 22-23, 29-32). So popular was Gideon that the people asked him to set up a dynasty, something altogether new for the nation of Israel. This was one way they could reward Gideon for what he had done for them. But it was also somewhat of a guarantee that there would be a measure of unity among the tribes as well as the kind of leadership that would mobilize them against possible future invaders.

Their request was a confession of unbelief; for as Gideon reminded them, *God* was their king.[4] Gideon rejected their generous offer purely on theological grounds: He would not take the place of Jehovah God. Every Jew should have known that the mercy seat in the tabernacle was the throne of God from which He ruled in the midst of His people. "You who sit enthroned between the cherubim, shine forth" (Ps. 80:1, NIV). "The Lord reigns, let the nations tremble; He sits enthroned between the cherubim, let the earth shake" (99:1, NIV). To set up a rival throne would be to dethrone the Lord.[5]

Moses warned that Israel would one day want a king like the other nations and forget that they were a unique nation, unlike the Gentiles (Deut. 4:5-8; 14:2; 17:14-20; Ex. 19:4-5). What other nation had the Creator, the Lord of heaven and earth, as their King?

What Gideon said was commendable, but what he did later on was very puzzling. After rejecting the throne, *he lived like a king!* Judges 8:29-32 describes the lifestyle of a monarch, not that of a judge or a retired army officer. Gideon was quite wealthy, partly from the spoils of battle and partly from the gifts of the people; and he had many wives and at least one concubine. His wives bore him seventy sons, his concubine bore him one. In fact, he named the son of the concubine Abimelech, which means "my father is a king"; and this son later tried to live up to his name and become ruler over all the land. Gideon also seems to have assumed priestly duties, for he made his own ephod and probably consulted it on behalf of the people.

Nobody would deny that this courageous soldier-judge deserved honor and rewards, but his "retirement plan" seemed a bit extravagant.

Gideon requests gold (vv. 24-28). The people were only too eager to share their spoils with Gideon. After all, he had brought peace to the land (v. 28)[6] and had refused to become their king. Therefore, it was only right that he receive something for his labors. The Midianites wore gold crescents, either on the ear or the nose (Gen. 24:47), and the Israelite soldiers would have quickly taken these valuable items as they gathered the spoils. Gideon ended up with over forty pounds of gold, plus the wealth he took from Zebah and Zalmunna. No wonder he was able to live like a king!

But at this point the man of faith led the people into idolatry; for Gideon made an ephod, and the people "played the harlot" with it (v. 27, NKJV). This meant that they stopped giving their true devotion to the Lord and used the ephod for an idol. In Scripture, idolatry is looked upon as prostitution (Isa. 50:1-3; 54:6-8; Jer. 2:1-3; 3:1ff; Hosea 2; James 4:4; Rev. 2:4). Gideon may have made the ephod as a representation of Jehovah, to "help the people" in their worship, but a good motive can never compensate for a bad action. He knew it was wrong to make an idol (Ex. 20:4-6).

Whether this ephod was an embellished version of the garment used by the high priest (28:6), or some kind of standing idol (see Jud. 17:5; 18:14, 17), we can't tell; but it was used in worship and became a snare to Gideon and the people (Ps. 106:36). Perhaps Gideon used it to determine the will of God and help the people with their problems. If the ephod was indeed a copy of the high priest's garment, then Gideon was definitely out of God's will in duplicating it and using it, because Gideon wasn't a priest. If it was a standing idol, Gideon was disobeying God's Law (Ex. 20:4-6) and corrupting the people as well, It was just a short step from worshiping the ephod to worshiping Baal (Jud. 8:33).

Gideon missed a great opportunity to bring reformation and perhaps revival to the land. He had torn down his father's idols, but there were many households in Israel that were still devoted to Baal, and those idols needed to be destroyed as well. The great victory over Midian gave Gideon good reason to call the nation back to the Lord and obedience to His Law. But instead of using the occasion for God's glory, he used it for his own profit; and the nation eventually lapsed into sin once again.

With his vast wealth and his great national reputation, Gideon probably thought that his children were well provided for, but just the opposite proved true. Sixty-nine of his seventy sons were killed by their half-brother who himself was slain by a woman dropping a stone on his head. *There is no security apart from the will of God.* Had Gideon practiced Matthew 6:33, subsequent events might have been radically different.

What caused Gideon's spiritual decline? I think it was pride. Before the battle against Midian, Gideon humbly depended on the Lord. During the "mopping up" operations, however, he became authoritative and even vindictive. When he refused the kingship, he sounded pious ("the Lord shall rule over you"), but I have a suspicion that he had a hidden agenda in his heart. You don't find Gideon honoring the Lord or calling the people together to make a new covenant to obey the Lord. Gideon started out as a servant, but now he was an important celebrity. The result was decline for him, his family, and his nation.

It's interesting and instructive to contrast Abraham and Gideon in the decisions they made after their respective victories (Gen. 14). Abraham took nothing for himself but made sure that others received their share of the spoils (Gen. 14:22-24). He especially refused to take anything from the heathen king of Sodom (Gen. 14:17, 21). Instead, Abraham fellowshipped with Melchizedek, King of Salem, a type of our Lord Jesus Christ (Heb. 7–8); and in all that he said and did, Abraham gave glory to the Lord of heaven and earth.

Andrew Bonar was right: "Let us be as watchful after the victory as before the battle." After all, there may still be some land mines scattered around!

My Kingdom Come

When George Washington's army defeated the British General Charles Cornwallis at Yorktown, the end of the Revolutionary War began. Winning the war didn't automatically end the problems that the colonies faced. Things became so bad economically that one of George Washington's colonels wrote Washington a secret letter, urging him to use his army to make himself king or dictator. To the colonel, this was the only way to get the affairs of the young nation under control. Washington rejected the plan, but with his popularity and power he probably could have become king if he had so desired.

Abimelech was just the opposite. He had such a passionate desire to be king that he allowed nothing to stand in his way, not even the lives of hundreds of innocent people. This is the longest chapter in the Book of Judges and one of the most depressing.[1] The chapter records three stages in Abimelech's political career.

1. Seizing the kingdom (Jud. 9:1-21)

Abimelech was the son of Gideon by a slave woman who lived with her father's family in Shechem (8:30-31; 9:18). His name means "my father is a king." Although Gideon had certainly lived like a king, he had still refused to establish a dynasty in Israel, but Abimelech felt that his father had made a mistake. After his father's death, Abimelech decided that *he* should be king, thus he moved from Ophrah to Shechem, where he started his campaign. In what he did, Abimelech broke several of God's laws and as a result brought destruction to himself and trouble to the people.[2]

Selfish ambition (vv. 1-2). "You shall not covet" is the last of the Ten Commandments (Ex. 20:17, NKJV), but breaking it is the first step toward breaking the other nine. Of itself, ambition isn't an evil thing, provided it's mixed with genuine humility and is controlled by the will of God. If it's God's wind that lifts you and you're soaring on wings that He's given you, then fly as high as He takes you. But if you manufacture both the wind and the wings, you're heading for a terrible fall.

"One can never consent to creep when one feels an impulse to soar," said Helen Keller; and her counsel is good, so long as the impulse to soar comes from the Lord. Selfish ambition destroys. "I will ascend into heaven!" turned an angel into the devil (Isa. 14:13, NKJV), and "Is not this great Babylon, that I have built" turned a king into an animal (Dan. 4:28-37, NKJV). If we exalt ourselves, God has many ways of bringing us down (Matt. 23:12).

The Jews had been acquainted with the people of Shechem since the days of the patriarchs (Gen. 12:6; 33:18-20; 34:1ff). Both Jews and Canaanites lived in Shechem during Abimelech's days, which explains why he started his campaign there. His mother was a Shechemite and his father was a Jew. Therefore, if Abimelech became king, he could represent both constituencies!

Abimelech had another plank in his political platform: The Canaanites in Shechem had no indebtedness to Gideon's sons, while Abimelech was definitely one of their own. Furthermore, which of Gideon's seventy sons should be chosen king and how would he be selected? Or would all seventy try to rule the land together? With this kind of logic, Abimelech enlisted the support of both his relatives and the men of the city; and now he was ready to move into action.

Idolatry (v. 4). "You shall have no other gods before Me" and "You shall not make for yourself any carved image" are the first and second of the Ten Commandments (Ex. 20:3-4, NKJV), and Abimelech broke them both. It's obvious that he was his own god and that he had no interest in God's will for the nation. His accepting money from the Baal worshipers to finance his crusade was a public announcement that he had renounced the God of Israel and was on the side of Baal.

But Abimelech had another god beside ambition and Baal, and that was *might.* With the tainted money from the heathen temple, he hired a group of no-account mercenaries who helped him gain and keep control over the people. These vile terrorists also assisted him in his evil plot to murder his seventy half brothers and remove every rival to the throne.

The Greek philosopher Plato said, "Might is right"; and three centuries later, the Roman philosopher Seneca wrote, "Might makes right."[3] The French novelist Joseph Joubert wrote seventeen centuries later, "Might and right govern everything in the world; might till right is ready." But when *might* is in the hands of selfish dictators, *right* rarely has a chance to get ready or to take over. Might seizes control and will hold it unless a stronger power overcomes and brings freedom. The Prophet Habakkuk described these people as "guilty men, whose own strength is their god" (Hab. 1:11, NIV).

Murder (v. 5). The sixth commandment, "You shall not murder" (Ex. 20:13, NKJV), was violated scores of times by Abimelech and his mercenaries, beginning in Ophrah with their slaughter of sixty-nine of Abimelech's seventy half brothers. Why didn't somebody stop these murderers and defend Gideon's family? Because the people of Israel had forgotten both the goodness of the Lord and the kindness of Gideon (Jud. 8:33-35). They had neither the conviction to be concerned nor the courage to intervene. It doesn't take long for society to change yesterday's hero into today's scoundrel. What the Irish poet William Butler Yeats described in his famous poem "The Second Coming" was true in the nation of Israel:

> The best lack all conviction, while the worst
> Are full of passionate intensity.

"Woe to him who builds a city with bloodshed and establishes a town by crime!" (Hab. 2:12, NIV) Revelation 21:8 and 22:15 make it clear that murderers go to hell. Of course, a murderer can call on the Lord and be saved just as any other sinner can, but there's no evidence that Abimelech and his crowd ever repented of their sins. Their feet were "swift to shed blood" (Rom. 3:15; Isa. 59:7), and the blood that they shed eventually came back on their own heads.

Murder is bad enough, but when brother kills brother, the sin is even more heinous. By murdering his half brothers, Abimelech joined the ranks of other men in the Bible who committed fratricide, including Cain (Gen. 4), Absalom (2 Sam. 13:23ff), and Jehoram (2 Chron. 21:4). Not very nice company.

Dishonesty (v. 6). The third commandment says, "You shall not take the name of the Lord your God in vain" (Ex. 20:7, NKJV), and the ninth commandment forbids us bearing false witness (Ex. 20:16). Abimelech broke both commandments when he was crowned king. If he took an oath of office in the name of the Lord, it was pure blasphemy; and if he promised

to protect the people and obey the law, it was further deception. (See Deut. 17:14-20.) No matter what he promised at
the coronation, Abimelech had his own agenda and intended
to carry it out.

The cynical journalist Ambrose Bierce defined "politics" as
"a strife of interests masquerading as a contest of principles;
the conduct of public affairs for private advantage." Certainly
history records the names of dedicated men and women who
put the good of their country ahead of the good of their party
and personal gain, but in the case of Abimelech, Bierce's
definition applies perfectly.

Abimelech's "coronation" was a farce, an empty ritual that
was never accepted or blessed by the Lord. The new "king"
not only blasphemed God by the promises he made, but he
defiled a place sacred in Jewish history. The coronation took
place at the "great tree at the pillar in Shechem" (Jud. 9:6,
NIV). This is probably the "oak of Moreh," where the Lord
appeared to Abraham and promised to give him and his descendants the land (Gen. 12:6). It was near this site that the
nation of Israel heard the blessings and curses read from the
Law and promised to obey the Lord (Deut. 11:26-32; Josh.
8:30-35). Jacob buried the idols here as he called his family
back to God (Gen. 35:1-5), and here Joshua gave his last
speech and led the people in reaffirming their obedience to
the Lord (Josh. 24:25-26). All of this sacred history was de-
graded and dishonored by the selfish acts of one godless man.

Pride (vv. 7-21). Jotham was the only brother to escape the
massacre (v. 5).[4] Perhaps the coronation celebrations were
still in progress when Jotham interrupted with his parable
from Mount Gerizim, which was adjacent to Shechem and the
oak of Moreh. It was from Mount Gerizim that the blessings
were to be read (Deut. 27:12, 28), but Jotham's story was
anything but a blessing. It's worth noting that the tribe of
Joseph (Ephraim and Manasseh) was to stand on the mount

of blessing; but Abimelech certainly hadn't brought any blessing to Gideon's tribe of Manasseh.

This is the first parable recorded in Scripture. Many people have the idea that Jesus invented parables and that they are found only in the four Gospels, but neither is the case. Besides this "Parable of the Trees," the Old Testament also contains Nathan's "Parable of the Ewe Lamb" (2 Sam. 12:1-4), the parable by the woman of Tekoa (2 Sam. 14:5-20), the Parable of the Thistle (2 Kings 14:8-14), and the Parable of the Vineyard (Isa. 5:1-7). The prophecies of Jeremiah and Ezekiel contain both standard parables as well as "action" parables (Jer. 13, 18-19, 27-28; Ezek. 4-5, 16, 31, etc.).

Jotham pictured the trees looking for a king.[5] They approached the olive tree with its valuable oil, the fig tree with its sweet fruit, and the vine with its clusters that could be made into wine; but all of them refused to accept the honor. They would each have to sacrifice something in order to reign, and they weren't prepared to make that sacrifice.

All that remained was the bramble, a thornbush that was a useless nuisance in the land, good only for fuel for the fire. This, of course, was a symbol of Abimelech, the new king. For a thornbush to invite the other trees to trust in its shadow is a laughable proposition indeed! Often in the summer, fires would break out in the bramble bushes; and these fires would spread and threaten the safety of the trees. (See David's use of this image in 2 Sam. 23:6-7, and also Isa. 9:18-19.)

Jotham had made his point: Abimelech, the "bramble king," would be unable to protect the people, but he would cause judgment to come that would destroy those who trusted him. The men of Shechem should have been ashamed of the way they rejected the house of Gideon and honored a worthless opportunist like Abimelech. Eventually, both Abimelech and his followers would destroy one another.

Abimelech considered himself to be a stately tree of great value, but Jotham said he was nothing but a useless weed. What a blow to the new king's pride! When they chose Abimelech as their king, the men of Shechem didn't get useful olive oil, tasty figs, or cheery wine; they got only thorns — fuel for the fire.

Abimelech was actually trying to wrest the kingdom away from God (Jud. 8:23), and the Lord permitted him to have a measure of success. But God was still on the throne and would see to it that man's selfish purposes would be frustrated.

It's a dangerous thing for us to think more highly of ourselves than we ought to think (Rom. 12:3). We all need to discover the gifts God has given us and then use them in the place where He puts us. Each member in the body of Christ is important (1 Cor. 12:12-31), and we all need one another and to minister to one another. Since there's no competition in the work of the Lord (John 4:34-38; 1 Cor. 3:5-9), there's no need for us to promote ourselves. The important thing is that God receives the glory.

2. Defending the kingdom (Jud. 9:22-29)

After three years of relative success, Abimelech found himself in trouble. It's one thing to acquire a throne and quite something else to defend and retain it. The citizens of Shechem, who had helped crown him king, began to give him trouble, as well as an intruder named Gaal. All of this was from the Lord, who was about to punish both Abimelech and the men of Shechem for the slaughter of Gideon's sons. "Though the mills of God grind slowly, yet they grind exceeding small" (Longfellow, *Retribution*).

The activities of at least three days are described in this section.

Day one — the boasting of Gaal (vv. 25-33). The Lord created a breech between the king and his followers, so much so that the Shechemites started to work against the king. They began to rob the caravans that passed by the city on the nearby trade routes. Abimelech was living at Arumah (v. 41), and the activities of these bandits were robbing him of both money and reputation. The merchants would hear about the danger, take a different trade route, and not have to pay Abimelech whatever tariffs were usually levied upon them. But even more, the word would get out that the new king couldn't control his people and protect area business.

Into this volatile situation stepped a newcomer, Gaal the son of Ebed, a man who knew a good opportunity when he saw it. In a short time, he gained the confidence of the men of Shechem, who were already unhappy with their king; and when a crowd was gathered to celebrate a harvest festival, Gaal openly criticized Abimelech's administration. He reminded the people that their king had a Jewish father, while they were sons of Hamor, not sons of Jacob (Gen. 34). The plank in Abimelech's platform that he thought was the strongest (v. 9) turned out to be his thorn in the flesh.

His approach in verse 29 was effective. Gaal was living in Shechem while Abimelech was living in Arumah. The people could tell Gaal their problems, and he could give them the help they needed, but how could they go to Arubah for help? Years later, Absalom would use this same approach and steal the hearts of Israel (2 Sam. 15:1-6). Gaal closed his festival address by saying, "I would say to Abimelech, 'Call out your whole army!' " (Jud. 9:29, NIV) It was a challenge that he dared the king to take up.

Abimelech's representative in Shechem was Zebul, who wasted no time getting the information about Gaal to the king. Not only did Zebul share the contents of the speech, but he also gave the king some strategy for dealing with this boastful intruder. Zebul would be working for the king within the city, and the king would gather his troops outside the city.

Day two — the defeat of Gaal (vv. 34-41). Abimelech used some of Gideon's strategy (v. 34), although he didn't have Gideon's faith or the weapons Gideon and his men used. You get the impression that Zebul had convinced Gaal that he was his friend, for Gaal actually believed the lie Zebul told him. As the two men stood by the gate early that morning, Abimelech was setting the trap and Zebul was going to put in the bait.

When it was obvious that an army was attacking Shechem, Gaal had to act. In the decisive words of American slang, he had to "put up or shut up." If he hid in the city, he would have lost his following, been disgraced, and eventually caught and killed. If he tried to run away, Abimelech's men would have chased him and killed him. All he could do was gather his followers and go out to face Abimelech. His army was routed, and he and his cohorts were driven out of the city.

Day three — the punishment of Shechem (vv. 42-49). Abimelech had one more score to settle, and that was with the citizens of Shechem who had cursed him (v. 27) and were attacking the caravans and robbing him of both money and reputation. The next morning, when the people of Shechem went out of the city to work in the fields, Abimelech set an ambush, blocked the city gate, and slaughtered the trapped citizens. Thus the Lord avenged the blood of Gideon's sons. Indeed, the fire did "come out of the bramble, and devour the cedars of Lebanon" (v. 15). The phrase "cedars of Lebanon" represents the leading citizens of the city, who had supported Abimelech's rule (v. 20).

In order to make sure the city didn't rebel against him again, Abimelech destroyed it and sowed salt over it. The sowing of salt on a conquered city was a symbolic action that condemned the city to desolation so nobody would want to live there. "Put salt on Moab, for she will be laid waste; her

towns will become desolate, with no one to live in them"
(Jer. 48:9, NIV; and see Jer. 17:6).

The "tower of Shechem" may have been the same as "the
house of Millo" mentioned in Judges 9:6. It was the place
where the aristocracy of Shechem lived, although we don't
know where it was located with reference to the main city.
The people fled from Beth-Millo to the temple of El-Berith
("god of the covenant"; Baal-Berith, v. 4, and see 8:33). Apparently they felt safer in a building devoted to one of their
gods, hoping that Abimelech would respect it and leave them
alone. But he turned the temple into a furnace and killed all
the people in it.

3. Losing the kingdom (Jud. 9:50-57)

The shedding of innocent blood is something that God takes
very seriously and eventually avenges (Deut. 19:10, 13; 21:9;
1 Kings 2:31; Prov. 6:17; Isa. 59:7; Jer. 7:6; 22:3, 17; Joel
3:19). The year 1990 was a record year for murders in the
United States, with 23,438 persons being killed, an average of
nearly three an hour all year long. When you add to this the
thousands of innocent babies killed in their mother's wombs,
it's easy to see that "the land of the free" is stained with
innocent blood; and one day we will pay for it.

Abimelech paid for the murders he committed, and it happened while he was attempting to protect his throne. Since
the people in the city of Thebez, about ten miles from Shechem, had apparently joined in the general rebellion against
Abimelech, he went there with his army to punish them as
well. Like the people from Beth-Millo, the citizens of Thebez
fled to their tower; and Abimelech tried to use the same
method of attack that he used so successfully at Shechem.

However, he made the mistake of getting too close to the
tower, and a woman dropped an upper millstone on his head
and killed him. Abimelech experienced a triple disgrace: (1)

He was killed, but not really in a battle; (2) he was killed by a woman, which was a disgrace to a soldier; and (3) he was killed with a millstone, not a sword. The fact that his armorbearer finished the job with a sword didn't change anything; for centuries later, Abimelech's shameful death was remembered as being accomplished by a woman (2 Sam. 11:21).

Abimelech lost his life and lost his kingdom. The curse pronounced by his half-brother Jotham was fulfilled on both Abimelech and the people of Shechem (Jud. 9:20). "Evil will slay the wicked; the foes of the righteous will be condemned" (Ps. 34:21, NIV). "The Righteous One takes note of the house of the wicked and brings the wicked to ruin" (Prov. 21:12, NIV).

Local Reject Makes Good

Life and literature are filled with the "Cinderella legend," stories about rejected people who were eventually "discovered" and elevated to places of honor and authority. Horatio Alger wrote over 100 boys' novels that focused on the "rags-to-riches" theme, and he became one of the most influential American writers of the last half of the nineteenth century. Whether it's Abraham Lincoln going "from log cabin to White House" or Joseph from the prison to the throne of Egypt, the story of the successful "underdog" is one that will always be popular. We like to see losers become winners.

The account of Jephthah, the main character in these chapters, is that kind of a story, except that it doesn't end with the hero living "happily ever after." After Jephthah's great victory over the Ammonites and Philistines, he experienced anything but happiness; and the narrative ends on a tragic note. The story can be divided into four scenes.

1. A nation in decay (Jud. 10:1-18)

There were three deficiencies in Israel that gave evidence that the nation was decaying spiritually.

Israel's lack of gratitude to the Lord (vv. 1-5). For forty-five

years, the people of Israel enjoyed peace and security, thanks
to the leadership of Tola and Jair. We know little about these
two judges, but the fact that they kept Israel's enemies away
for nearly half a century would suggest that they were faithful
men, who served the Lord and the nation well. Tola was from
the tribe of Issachar, and Jair from the Transjordan tribes, the
area known as Gilead.

If Jair had thirty sons, he must have had a plurality of wives
and a great deal of wealth. In that day, only wealthy people
could afford to provide their children with their own personal
donkeys (5:10; 12:9, 14). In addition, each son had a city
under his authority. This arrangement looks to us like nepo-
tism, but at least it helped keep the peace.

The people of Israel, however, didn't take advantage of
these years of peace to grow in their relationship to the Lord.
After the death of Jair, the nation openly returned to idolatry
and once again invited the chastening of the Lord. *They enjoyed forty-five years of peace and prosperity but didn't take time
to thank the Lord for what He had done for them.* The essence
of idolatry is enjoying God's gifts but not being grateful to the
Giver, and Israel was guilty.

One of my great-uncles was a minister; and he occasionally
had Sunday dinner in our home if he happened to be preach-
ing at the church we attended. As a lad, I was impressed by
him, especially the way he asked the blessing *after* the meal.
Praying *before* the meal was logical and biblical, but why pray
after you've finished dessert and coffee? Then I discovered
Deuteronomy 8:10, "When you have eaten and are full, then
you shall bless the Lord your God for the good land which He
has given you" (NKJV). My Uncle Simon took this admonition
seriously, and perhaps we should follow his example. If we
did, it might keep us from ignoring the Lord while enjoying
His blessings. Thanksgiving glorifies God (Ps. 69:30) and is a
strong defense against selfishness and idolatry.

Israel's lack of submission to the Lord (vv. 6-16). If the people had only reviewed their own history and learned from it, they would never have turned from Jehovah God to worship the false gods of their neighbors. From the time of Othniel to the days of Gideon, the Jews endured over fifty painful years of oppression from the enemy. By now they should have known that God blessed them when they were obedient and chastened them when they were rebellious. (See 3:7, 12; 4:1; 6:1.) After all, weren't these the terms of the covenant that God made with Israel, a covenant the nation accepted when they entered the land? (Josh. 8:30-35)

When God chastens us in love and we're suffering because of our sins, it's easy to cry out to Him for deliverance and make all kinds of promises. But when we're comfortable and enjoying His blessings, we tend to forget God and assume that we can sin and get away with it. *Comfortable living often produces weak character.* "Happiness is not the end of life," said Henry Ward Beecher, "character is." But character is built when we make right decisions in life, and those decisions are made on the basis of the things that we value most. Since Israel didn't value the things of God, she ended up destroying her own national character.

The Lord had given Israel victory over seven different nations (Jud. 10:11-12), but now Israel was worshiping seven different varieties of pagan gods (v. 6). No wonder God's anger "was hot against Israel" (v. 7). What foolishness to worship the gods of your defeated enemies! Israel had to be chastened again, and this time God sent the Philistines and the Ammonites to do the job. The Ammonites were distant relatives of the Jews, being descendants of Abraham's nephew Lot (Gen. 19:38). It must have given the leaders of Ammon and Philistia great joy to subdue their old enemy Israel and oppress them. Their armies invaded the area of Gilead on the east side of the Jordan and then crossed the river and attacked Judah, Ephraim, and Benjamin. It was a devastating and humiliating conquest.

History repeated itself, and the Israelites cried out to God for deliverance (Jud. 10:10; 2:11-19). But the Lord didn't send help immediately. Instead, He sent a messenger to the people who rebuked them for their lack of appreciation for all that God had done for them in the past. Then God announced that He wouldn't help them anymore. They could ask their new gods for help! (See Deut. 32:36-38.)

For the people to abandon God was one thing, but for God to abandon His people was quite something else. *The greatest judgment God can send to His people is to let them have their own way and not interfere.* "Wherefore God also gave them up. . . . God gave them up. . . . God gave them over" (Rom. 1:24, 26, 28). This was too much for the Jews, so they repented, put away their false gods, and told God He could do to Israel whatever He wanted to do (Jud. 10:15-16).

Their hope wasn't in their repenting or their praying but in the character of God. "His soul was grieved for the misery of Israel" (v. 16). "In all their affliction He was afflicted" (Isa. 63:9). "Nevertheless in Your great mercy You did not utterly consume them nor forsake them; for You are God, gracious and merciful" (Neh. 9:31, NKJV). "Yet He was merciful; He atoned for their iniquities and did not destroy them. Time after time He restrained His anger and did not stir up His full wrath" (Ps. 78:38, NIV).

Israel's lack of adequate leadership (vv. 17-18). The people were prepared to act, but from all the tribes of Israel, there was nobody to take the lead. Whether in a nation or a local church, the absence of qualified leaders is often a judgment of God and evidence of the low spiritual level of the people. When the Spirit is at work among believers, He will equip and call servants to accomplish His will and bless His people (Acts 13:1-4).

In his book *Profiles in Courage,* John F. Kennedy wrote, "We, the people, are the boss, and we will get the kind of political leadership, be it good or bad, that we demand and deserve."[1] What's true of political leadership is often true of spiritual leadership: We get what we deserve. When God's people are submitted to Him and serving Him, He sends them gifted servants to instruct and lead them; but when their appetites turn to things of the world and the flesh, He judges them by depriving them of good and godly leaders. "The righteous perish, and no one ponders it in his heart" (Isa. 57:1, NIV).

After eighteen years of suffering, the Israelites assembled to face their oppressors (Jud. 10:11). There are several places in Scripture named "Mizpah"; this one was in Gilead (11:29; see Josh. 13:26). Israel had an army, but they didn't have a general. In order to get a volunteer to command their army, the leaders of Israel promised that their commander would be named head over all Gilead. Had the princes of Israel called a prayer meeting instead of a political caucus, they would have accomplished more.

When I was a young Christian, I heard an evangelist preach a powerful sermon on the text, "Where is the Lord God of Elijah?" (2 Kings 2:14) "We know where the Lord God of Elijah is," he said; "He's on the throne of heaven and is just as powerful today as He was in Elijah's day." Then he paused. "The question is not so much 'Where is the Lord God of Elijah?' as 'Where are the Elijahs?' "

Indeed, *where are the Elijahs?* Where are the spiritual leaders who can rally God's people and confront the forces of evil?

2. A leader in demand (Jud. 11:1-29, 32-33)

Now we are introduced to Jephthah, the man God chose to lead Israel to victory. What kind of man was he?

The unwanted brother (vv. 1-3). Jephthah wasn't to blame for his birth. His father Gilead had only one wife, but he consorted with a prostitute and fathered a son. At least Gilead acknowledged the boy and took him into his home, but his other sons didn't accept this "son of a strange woman." When Gilead died and the inheritance was to be divided, the legitimate sons drove Jephthah away. Little did they realize they were rejecting a future judge of Israel.

Jephthah left his father's territory and went north to the land of Tob, which was near Syria; and there he became captain of a band of "adventurers" (v. 3, NIV). The Hebrew word means "to make empty" and refers to idle people looking for something to do. (See 9:4, the "vain and light persons" who followed Abimelech. Here the word means "to be reckless.") Jephthah was already known as "a mighty man of valour" (v. 1). Thus he had no trouble forming a band of brigands.

The unopposed leader (vv. 4-11). Jephthah's brothers didn't want him, but the elders of Israel needed him and sent a deputation eighty miles to the land of Tob to ask him to take charge. Jephthah's reply sounds a good deal like what the Lord had said to the people when they turned to Him for help (10:13-14). Apparently the Jewish leaders had cooperated with Gilead's sons in expelling the unwanted brother from the land, but Jephthah listened to them and made sure their offer was valid. He was willing to lead them against the enemy if the elders would name him ruler of Gilead.

You can't help but appreciate the way Jephthah emphasized the Lord in all his negotiations with the leaders of Israel. It was the Lord who would give the victory (11:9), not Jephthah; and the agreement between him and the elders must be ratified before the Lord at Mizpah (v. 11; see 1 Sam. 11:15). Jephthah didn't see the challenge as a political opportunity for himself but as an occasion for trusting the Lord and serving

Him. In addition, the writer of Hebrews makes it clear that Jephthah was a man of faith, not simply an opportunist (Heb. 11:32).

We can't help but wonder how his brothers felt when the man they renounced returned home as the captain of the army and the leader of the land! More than one "underdog" in Scripture had the same experience. Joseph was rejected by his brothers and later became their savior. It also took King David seven years to gain the full support of the twelve tribes of Israel. For that matter, the Lord Jesus Christ was rejected by His people but will be received by them when He comes again.

The unsuccessful diplomat (vv. 12-28). Before declaring war, Jephthah tried peaceful negotiations with the Ammonites, but the negotiations failed. Nevertheless, this section does tell us two things about Jephthah: (1) He knew the Scriptures and the history of his people, and (2) he was not a hothead who was looking for a fight. Being a military man himself, Jephthah knew that a war could result in thousands of Jewish men being killed; and he wanted to avoid that if at all possible.

The King of Ammon declared that he and his men were only reclaiming land that the Jews, under the leadership of Moses, had stolen from them. If Israel would restore that land, he would call off his troops. But Jephthah presented four compelling arguments that should have convinced the Ammonites that they were wrong.

First, he presented the facts of history (vv. 14-22). Moses and his people had asked the Ammonites for safe passage through their territory, a request that the Ammonites would not grant. This led to war, and God gave the Jews the victory. Israel didn't *steal* any land; they *captured* it from the Ammonites and the Amorites (Num. 21:21-35). Furthermore, the Amorites had originally taken the land from the Moabites (Num. 21:29); so if Israel's claims to ownership by conquest weren't valid, neither were the claims of the Amorites!

His second argument was that the Lord had given Israel the land (vv. 23-24). Jephthah was always careful to give the Lord the glory for any victories Israel won (vv. 9, 21, 23-24). When the other nations captured enemy territory, they claimed that it was "the will of their god" that they take the land; and they gave their idols credit for the victory. Jephthah declared that the God of Israel was the true God and that His will had been fulfilled in allowing Israel to take the land. It was Jehovah who gave Israel the victory.

Jephthah's third argument was that Israel had lived on the land for centuries (vv. 25-26). "Three hundred years" is a round figure, but it comes close to the total number of years given in the Book of Judges for the periods of oppression and of peace. Israel had dwelt in the Transjordan area for three centuries, and that was reason enough to claim title to the land as their own. Why was the King of Ammon making his claims now? During those three centuries, the people of Ammon didn't try to reclaim their territory. In fact, back in the days of Moses, even the King of Moab hadn't tried to get his land back! If the Ammonites had a legitimate claim to the territory, they should have said something centuries ago!

Jephthah's final argument was that the Ammonites were actually fighting against the Lord (vv. 27-28). Jephthah hadn't declared war on Ammon; it was Ammon that declared war on Israel. But if God gave Israel the land, then the Ammonites were declaring war on the Lord God; and that could only mean disaster and defeat for Ammon. Jephthah had tried to reason with the King of Ammon, but he wouldn't listen.

The undefeated warrior (vv. 29-33). Empowered by the Spirit of God (see 3:10; 6:34), Jephthah called for volunteers (12:1-2) and mustered his army. In order to be certain of victory, he foolishly made a bargain with God, a subject we shall take up later. The Lord gave him victory over the

Ammonites, and he captured twenty of their strongholds as he pursued the fleeing enemy army. This would guarantee freedom and safety for the Jews as they traveled in the Gilead territory.

The writer of Hebrews wrote that Jephthah was a man of faith and his victory was a victory of faith (Heb. 11:32). *The circumstances of birth or of family are not a handicap to the person who will live by faith.* In his message to the King of Ammon, Jephthah revealed his knowledge of the Word of God; and this Word was the source of His faith. "So then faith comes by hearing, and hearing by the Word of God" (Rom. 10:17, NKJV). "And this is the victory that has overcome the world—our faith" (1 John 5:4, NKJV). Thanks to the faith and courage of Jephthah, the Ammonites didn't threaten the Israelites for another fifty years (1 Sam. 11:1ff).

3. A father in despair (Jud. 11:30-31, 34-40)

While going out to battle, Jephthah made a vow to the Lord. It was certainly acceptable to God for the Jews to make vows, provided they obeyed the laws that He had given through Moses to govern the use of vows (Lev. 27; Num. 30; Deut. 23:21-25). Vows were completely voluntary, but the Lord expected the people to fulfill them (Ecc. 5:1-6).

Jephthah's vow was really a bargain with the Lord: If God would give the Israelites victory over the Ammonites, Jephthah would sacrifice to the Lord whatever came out of his house when he arrived home in Mizpah. God did give him victory, and Jephthah kept his promise. But what was his promise and how did he keep it? What actually happened to Jephthah's daughter, his only child?

The vow. The *Authorized (King James) Version* reads: "If Thou shalt without fail deliver the children of Ammon into mine hands, then it shall be, that whatsoever cometh forth of the doors of my house to meet me, when I return in peace from the children of Ammon, shall surely be the Lord's, and I will offer it up for a burnt offering" (Jud. 11:30-31).

The *New American Standard Bible* translates this verse to say, "If Thou wilt indeed give the sons of Ammon into my hand, then it shall be that whatever comes out of the doors of my house to meet me when I return in peace from the sons of Ammon, it shall be the Lord's, and I will offer it up as a burnt offering."

The *New International Version* translates it to say, "If You give the Ammonites into my hands, whatever comes out of the door of my house to meet me when I return in triumph from the Ammonites will be the Lord's, and I will sacrifice it as a burnt offering."

The questions. The more you study Jephthah's vow, the more puzzling it becomes. He simply could have said, "Lord, if You help me defeat the enemy, when I get home, I'll offer you a generous burnt offering." But he couched his vow in ambiguous terms. How did he know who or what would come out of the door of his house? What if the first thing to greet him happened to be an unclean animal that was unacceptable to God? Then he couldn't fulfill his vow! The Hebrew word translated "whatsoever" (KJV) or "whatever" (NASB) is masculine and suggests that he expected to meet a person,[2] but what if that person turned out to be a neighbor's child or a total stranger? What right did Jephthah have to take either life and thereby offer to God a sacrifice that cost him nothing? (See 2 Sam. 24:24.)

Furthermore, surely Jephthah knew that Jehovah didn't approve of or accept human sacrifices. Jephthah gave evidence of familiarity with the Old Testament Scriptures, and he would have known about Abraham and Isaac (Gen. 22) and the commandments in the Law (Lev. 18:21 and 20:1-5; Deut. 12:31 and 18:10). Granted, the period of the Judges was a spiritually dark era in Israel's history, and the Jews did many things that were wrong, but it's doubtful that Jephthah's friends and neighbors would have permitted him to slay his own daughter in order to fulfill a foolish vow.[3] King Saul's soldiers didn't let him kill his son Jonathan, who had violated his father's foolish vow (1 Sam. 14:24-46).

And where would Jephthah offer his daughter as a sacrifice? Surely he knew that the Lord accepted sacrifices only at the tabernacle altar (Lev. 17:1-9), and that they had to be offered by the levitical priests. He would have to travel to Shiloh to fulfill his vow (Deut. 16:2, 6, 11, 16), and it's doubtful that even the most unspiritual priest would offer a human sacrifice on God's sanctified altar, victory or no victory.[4] In fact, if people knew that Jephthah was going to Shiloh to slay his daughter, they probably would have stopped him along the way and kidnapped the girl! A national hero like Jephthah couldn't easily hide what he was doing, and surely the story would have spread quickly among the people during the two-month waiting period (Jud. 11:37-39).

But even if he made it safely to Shiloh, Jephthah could have learned from any priest that paying the proper amount of money could have redeemed his daughter (Lev. 27:1-8). As a successful soldier who had just returned from looting the enemy, Jephthah could easily have paid the redemption price.

Other pertinent questions arise. In spite of Numbers 30:1-2, would God take seriously a vow that violated both human rights and divine law? Would a Spirit-empowered man (Jud. 11:29), committed to the Lord (11:11), even make such a vow? The more I ponder these questions, the more perplexing his vow becomes and the more convinced I am that Jephthah didn't promise to offer any human sacrifice to the Lord and did not kill his own daughter.

Solutions. More than one expositor has pointed out that the little word "and" in the phrase "and I will offer it up" (11:31) can be translated "or." (In the Hebrew, it's the letter *waw* which usually means "and." See the beginning of Ps. 119:41 for an example of what the Hebrew *waw* looks like.) If we take this approach, then the vow was twofold: Whatever met him when he returned home would be dedicated to the Lord (if a person) *or* sacrificed to the Lord (if an animal).

Since he was met by his daughter, Jephthah gave her to the Lord to serve Him at the tabernacle (Ex. 38:8; 1 Sam. 2:22). She remained a virgin, which meant that she would not know the joys of motherhood and perpetuate her father's inheritance in Israel. This would be reason enough for her and her friends to spend two months grieving, for every daughter wanted a family and every father wanted grandchildren to maintain the family inheritance.

Nowhere in the text are we told that Jephthah actually killed his daughter, nor do we find anybody bewailing the girl's death. The emphasis in Judges 11:37-40 is the fact that she remained a virgin. It's difficult to believe that "the daughters of Israel" would establish a custom to celebrate (not "lament" as in KJV) the awful sacrifice of a human being, but we can well understand that they would commemorate the devotion and obedience of Jephthah's daughter in helping her father fulfill his vow. She deserves to stand with Isaac as a faithful child, who was willing to obey both father and God, no matter what the cost.[5]

4. A ruler in defense (Jud. 12:1-15)

Accusation (v. 1). The leaders of the tribe of Ephraim expressed to Jephthah the same pride and anger they had shown to Gideon (8:1). As before, they wanted to share the glory of the victory, but they hadn't been too eager to risk their lives in the battle. The men of Ephraim were so angry that they threatened to burn Jephthah's house down. They had absolutely no respect for the new ruler of the Transjordanic tribes.

Explanation (vv. 2-3). Gideon had pacified the Ephraimites with flattery, but Jephthah took a more direct approach. To begin with, he reminded them that his first concern was to defeat the Ammonites, not to please his neighbors. Second, during the eighteen years Ammon had oppressed the people of Gilead, nobody from Ephraim had offered to come to their rescue. Third, Jephthah had issued a call for the tribes to assist him in his attack on the enemy, but Ephraim hadn't responded. Without their help, the Lord gave Jephthah and his army victory; so the proud Ephraimites (who didn't like being left out) had nothing to complain about.

Confrontation (vv. 4-7). Perhaps Jephthah should have practiced Proverbs 15:1 and 17:14 and avoided a war; but then, maybe it was time somebody called Ephraim's bluff and taught them a lesson. The men of Ephraim resorted to name-calling and taunted the Gileadites by calling them "renegades from Ephraim and Manasseh" (Jud. 12:4, NIV). Actually, the tribes east of the Jordan River—Reuben, Gad, and half of the tribe of Manasseh—had been granted their land by Moses and Joshua (Num. 32; Josh. 22). Thus the words of the Ephraimites were an insult to the Lord and His servants.

When people are wrong and refuse to accept logical reasoning and confess their faults, they often turn to violence in order to protect their reputation. This is the cause of most family disagreements, church fights, and international conflicts (James 4:1-12). But Jephthah got the best of the boastful men of Ephraim and killed 42,000 of their soldiers. The men of Ephraim themselves became "renegades," for the word "escaped" in Judges 12:5 is the same as the word "fugitives [renegades]" in verse 4. They had to eat their words *and* lose their lives!

The people of Ephraim had their own regional pronunciation for the word *shibboleth,* which means "stream" or "floods." They said "sibboleth," and this gave them away

(Matt. 26:73). It was a simple test, but it worked. Because of this story, the word *shibboleth* has become a part of our English vocabulary and is now found in our dictionaries. It stands for any kind of test that a group gives to outsiders to see whether they really belong. Usually the *shibboleth* is an old worn-out idea or doctrine that is really unimportant. In Ephraim's case, however, it cost 42,000 people their lives.

After the defeat of Ammon and the trouncing of Ephraim, the Jews had thirty-one years of peace and security under the leadership of Jephthah and his three successors. How paradoxical that Jephthah the champion should have no family while Ibzan had thirty sons and thirty daughters and Abdon had forty sons and thirty grandsons.

Samson, however, the last judge God sent to His people, was the most paradoxical man of them them all: a deliverer who couldn't deliver himself, a conqueror who couldn't conquer himself, a strong man who didn't know when he was weak.

The Light That Flickered

It is a riddle wrapped up in a mystery inside an enigma."
In a speech broadcast October 1, 1939 that's how Sir
Winston Churchill described the actions of the Russians in
his day. But what he said about Russian actions could be
applied to Samson, the last of the judges, for his behavior is
"a riddle wrapped up in a mystery inside an enigma."

Samson was unpredictable and undependable because he
was double-minded, and "a double-minded man is unstable in
all his ways" (James 1:8). It has well been said that "the
greatest ability is dependability," and you could depend on
Samson to be undependable.

Bold before men, Samson was weak before women and
couldn't resist telling them his secrets. Empowered by the
Spirit of God, he yielded his body to the appetites of the flesh.
Called to declare war on the Philistines, he fraternized with
the enemy and even tried to marry a Philistine woman. He
fought the Lord's battles by day and disobeyed the Lord's
commandments by night. Given the name Samson, which
means "sunny," he ended up in the darkness, blinded by the
very enemy he was supposed to conquer.

Four chapters in the Book of Judges are devoted to the

history of Samson. In Judges 13–14, we're introduced to "Sunny" and his parents, and we see the light flickering as Samson plays with sin. In Judges 15–16, the light goes out and Samson dies a martyr under the ruins of a heathen temple, a sad end to a promising life.[1]

Let's open Samson's family album and study three pictures of Samson taken early in his career.

1. The child with unbelievable promise (Jud. 13:1-23)

Consider the great promise that was wrapped up in this person named Samson.

He had a nation to protect (v. 1). With monotonous regularity we've read this phrase in the Book of Judges (3:7, 12; 4:1-2; 6:1; 10:6-7), and here it appears for the last time. It introduces the longest period of oppression that God sent to His people, forty years of Philistine domination.

The Philistines[2] were among the "sea people" who, in the twelfth century B.C., migrated from an area of Greece to the coastal plain of Canaan. The Jews weren't able to occupy that territory during their conquest of the land (Josh. 13:1-2). As you study your map, you'll note that their national life focused around the five key cities of Ashdod, Gaza, Ashkelon, Gath, and Ekron (1 Sam. 6:17). The land between Israel's hill country and the coastal plain was called the "Shephelah," which means "low country"; and it separated Philistia from Israel. Samson was born in Zorah, a city in Dan near the Philistine border; and he often crossed that border either to serve God or satisfy his appetites.

Samson judged Israel "in the days of the Philistines" (Jud. 15:20), which means that his twenty years in office were *during* the forty years of Philistine rule. Dr. Leon Wood dates the beginning of the Philistine oppression about 1095 B.C. and the end in 1055 B.C. with Israel's victory at Mizpeh (1 Sam. 7). About the middle of this period occurred the battle of

Aphek when Israel was ignominiously defeated by the Philistines and lost the ark and three priests (1 Sam. 4). Dr. Wood suggests that Samson's judgeship started about the time of the tragedy at Aphek and that his main job was to harass the Philistines and keep them from successfully overrunning the land and menacing the people.[3]

It's worth noting that there is no evidence given in the text that Israel cried out to God for deliverance at any time during the forty years of Philistine domination. The Philistines disarmed the Jews (1 Sam. 13:19-23) and therefore had little fear of a rebellion. Judges 15:9-13 indicates that the Jews were apparently content with their lot and didn't want Samson to "rock the boat." It's frightening how quickly we can get accustomed to bondage and learn to accept the *status quo*. Had the Philistines been more severe on the Jews, perhaps the Jews would have prayed to Jehovah for help.

Unlike most of the previous judges, Samson didn't deliver his people from foreign domination but he began the work of deliverance that others would finish (13:5). As a powerful and unpredictable hero, Samson frightened and troubled the Philistines (16:24) and kept them from devastating Israel as the other invading nations had done. But it would take the prayers of Samuel (1 Sam. 7) and the conquests of David (2 Sam. 5:17-25) to finish the job that Samson started and give Israel complete victory over the Philistines.

He had a God to serve (vv. 2-5). The tribe of Dan was originally assigned the land adjacent to Judah and Benjamin, extending to the Mediterranean Sea (Josh. 19:40-48). Since the Danites weren't able to dislodge the coastal inhabitants, however, the tribe relocated and moved north (Jud. 18–19), although some of the people remained in their original location. Zorah is about fifteen miles from Jerusalem in the foothill country near the border of Philistia.

When God wants to do something really great in His world,

He doesn't send an army but an angel. The angel often visits a couple and promises to send them a baby. His great plan of salvation got underway when He called Abraham and Sarah and gave them Isaac. When He wanted to deliver Israel from Egyptian bondage, God sent baby Moses to Amram and Jochebed (Ex. 6:20); and when in later years Israel desperately needed revival, God gave baby Samuel to Hannah (1 Sam. 1). When the fullness of time arrived, God gave Baby Jesus to Mary; and that baby grew up to die on the cross for the sins of the world.

Babies are fragile, but God uses the weak things of the world to confound the mighty (1 Cor. 1:26-28). Babies must have time to grow up, but God is patient and is never late in accomplishing His will. Each baby God sends is a gift from God, a new beginning, and carries with it tremendous potential. What a tragedy that we live in a society that sees the unborn baby as a menace instead of a miracle, an intruder instead of an inheritance.

We have every reason to believe the "angel of the Lord" who visited Manoah's wife was Jesus Christ, the Son of God (see Gen. 22:1-18; 31:11-13; Ex. 3:1-6; Jud. 6:11-24). Like Sarah (Gen. 18:9-15), Hannah (1 Sam. 1), and Elizabeth (Luke 1:5-25), Manoah's wife was barren and never expected to have a child. Since it would be the mother who would have the greatest influence on the child, both before and after birth, the angel solemnly charged her what to do.

Like John the Baptist, Samson would be a Nazirite from his mother's womb (Luke 1:13-15).[4] The word *Nazirite* comes from a Hebrew word that means "to separate, to consecrate." Nazirites were persons who, for a stated period of time, consecrated themselves to the Lord in a special way. They abstained from drinking wine and strong drink; they avoided touching dead bodies; and as a mark of their consecration, they allowed their hair to grow. The laws governing the Nazirite vow are given in Numbers 16.⁵

Manoah's wife had to be careful what she ate and drank because her diet would influence her unborn Nazirite son and could defile him. It's too bad every expectant mother doesn't exercise caution; for in recent years, the news media have informed us of the sad consequences babies suffer when their mothers use tobacco, alcohol, and narcotics during a pregnancy. Samson's Nazirite vow wasn't something he voluntarily took: God gave it to him; and his mother was a part of the vow of dedication. Not only was she to avoid anything related to the grape, but also she was to avoid foods that were unclean to the Jews (Lev. 11; Deut. 14:3-20).

Ordinarily, a Nazirite vow was for a limited period of time; but in Samson's case, the vow was to last all his life (Jud. 13:7). This was something Manoah and his wife would have to teach their son, and they would also have to explain why they didn't cut his hair. The claims of God were upon this child, and it was the obligation of the parents to train him for the work God sent him to do.

He had a home to honor (vv. 6-23). Manoah's wife immediately told her husband about the stranger's visit and message, although neither of them yet knew that the visitor was the Lord (v. 16). Manoah assumed that he was "a man of God," perhaps a visiting prophet; and he prayed that the Lord would send the man back. We can't help but be impressed with the devotion of this husband and wife to each other and to the Lord. The time of the Judges was one of apostasy and anarchy, but there were still Jewish homes that were dedicated to the Lord and that believed in prayer; and God was still working through them.

God answered Manoah's prayer and gave him an opportunity to ask an important question, which the angel of the Lord never answered: "When your words are fulfilled, what is to be the rule for the boy's life and work?" (v. 12, NIV) The Old

Testament Law not only gave instructions concerning Nazirites and clean and unclean foods, but also it told parents how to raise their children (Deut. 6). It wasn't necessary for the Lord to give Manoah and his wife additional instructions when the Word of God already told them what to do. The messenger simply repeated the warning he had already given to Manoah's wife.

Wanting to be a good and appreciative host, Manoah asked the guest to wait while he and his wife prepared a meal for him (6:18-19; Gen. 18:1-8). The stranger's cryptic reply was that he wouldn't eat their food but would permit them to offer a burnt offering to the Lord. After all, their promised son was a gift from God, and they owed the Lord their worship and thanks.

But Manoah thought to himself, *If I can't honor this man of God now, perhaps I can do it in the future after his words come true and the baby boy has been born.* (Note that Manoah believed the announcement and said "when" and not "if.") Manoah would have to know the man's name so he could locate him nine months later, but the man wouldn't tell his name except to say it was "wonderful." (See Gen. 32:29.) This is the same word used to name the Messiah in Isaiah 9:6; it is translated "wondrously" in Judges 13:19 of KJV, (NIV says "an amazing thing").

Ordinarily, Jewish worshipers had to bring their offerings to the tabernacle altar at Shiloh; but since the "man of God" commanded Manoah to offer the burnt offering, it was permissible to do it there, using a rock as the altar. Suddenly, the visitor ascended to heaven in the flame! Only then did Manoah and his wife discover that their visitor was an angel from the Lord. This frightened Manoah, because the Jews believed that nobody could look up on God and live (see 6:19-23). Using common sense, Manoah's wife convinced him that they couldn't die and fulfill God's promises at the same time.

Every baby born into a godly home carries the responsibility of honoring the family name. Samson's inconsistent life brought shame to his father's house just as it brought shame to the name of the Lord. Samson's relatives had to pull his body out of the wreckage of the Philistine temple and take it home for burial (16:31). In one sense, it was a day of victory over God's enemies; but it was also a day of defeat for Samson's family.

2. The champion with undefeatable power (Jud. 13:24-25)

The baby was born and was named Samson, which means "sunny" or "brightness." Certainly he brought light and joy to Manoah and his wife, who thought they would never have a family; and he also began to bring light to Israel during the dark days of Philistine oppression. While other judges were said to be clothed with God's Spirit (3:10; 6:34; 11:29), only of Samson is it said "the Lord blessed him" (13:24; see Luke 1:80 and 2:52). The hand of God was on him in a special way.

The secret of Samson's great strength was his Nazirite vow, symbolized by his unshorn hair (Jud. 16:17); and the source of that strength was the Holy Spirit of God (13:25; 14:6, 19; 15:14). We aren't told that Samson's physique was especially different from that of other men, although he may have resembled the strong men pictured in Bible storybooks. Perhaps it was as he entered his teen years, when a Jewish boy became a "son of the law," that he began to demonstrate his amazing ability.

Only a few of Samson's great feats are recorded in the Book of Judges: killing the lion bare-handed (14:5-6); slaying thirty Philistines (v. 19); catching 300 foxes (or jackals) and tying torches to their tails (15:3-5); breaking bonds (15:14; 16:9, 12, 14); slaying 1,000 men with the jawbone of a donkey (15:15); carrying off the Gaza city gate (16:3); and destroying the Philistine building (v. 30). Judges 16:24 indicates that he had done many more feats than those listed above, feats that had aggravated the Philistine people.

As you ponder the record of Samson's life, you get the impression that he was a fun-loving fellow with a good sense of humor; and sometimes he didn't take his gifts and his work seriously. A sense of humor is a good thing to have, but it must be balanced with serious devotion to the things of the Lord. "Serve the Lord with fear, and rejoice with trembling" (Ps. 2:11). Samson's power was a weapon to fight with and a tool to build with, not a toy to play with.

Notice another thing: Samson was a loner; unlike previous judges, he never "rallied the troops" and tried to unite Israel in throwing off the Philistine yoke. For twenty years he played the champion, but he failed to act the leader. Joseph Parker said that Samson was "an elephant in strength [but] a babe in weakness." We might add that, when it came to national leadership, he was a lost sheep!

3. The man with unreliable character (Jud. 14:1-20)

According to Hebrews 11:32, Samson was a man of faith, but he certainly wasn't a faithful man. He wasn't faithful to his parents' teaching, his Nazirite vow, or the laws of the Lord. It didn't take long for Samson to lose almost everything the Lord had given him, except his great strength; and he finally lost that as well.

He lost his respect for his parents (vv. 1-4). The Lord had given Samson a godly heritage, and he had been raised to honor the Lord; but when Samson fell in love, he wouldn't listen to his parents when they warned him. Samson had wandered four miles into enemy territory where he was captivated by a Philistine woman and decided to marry her. This, of course, was contrary to God's Law (Ex. 34:12-16; Deut. 7:1-3; and see 2 Cor. 6:14-18).

Samson was living by sight and not by faith. He was controlled by "the lust of the eyes" (1 John 2:16) rather than by the Law of the Lord. The important thing to Samson was not pleasing the Lord, or even pleasing his parents, but pleasing himself (Jud, 14:3, 7, see 2 Cor. 5:14-15).[6]

When God isn't permitted to rule in our lives, He overrules and works out His will in spite of our decisions. Of course, we're the losers for rebelling against Him; but God will accomplish His purposes either with us or in spite of us (Es. 4:10-14). Samson should have been going to a war instead of to a wedding, but God used this event to give Samson occasion to attack the enemy. Because of this event, Samson killed thirty men (Jud. 14:19), burned up the enemy crops (15:1-5), slaughtered a great number of Philistines (vv. 7-8), and slew 1,000 men (v. 15). Samson hadn't planned these things, but God worked them out just the same.

He lost his Nazirite separation (vv. 5-9). When Samson and his parents went down to Timnah to make arrangements for the marriage, it appears that Samson left the main road (and his parents) and went on a detour into the vineyards; and there a lion attacked him. A vineyard was a dangerous place for a man who was not supposed to have anything to do with grapes (Num. 6:1-4). Did God send the lion as a warning to Samson that he was walking on the wrong path? The Holy Spirit gave Samson power to defeat the enemy, but Samson persisted on his path of disobedience into enemy territory and an unlawful wedding.

Some weeks later, when Samson returned to claim his bride, he once again turned aside into the vineyard, this time to look at his trophy and perhaps gloat over his victory. His sin began with "the lust of the flesh" and "the lust of the eyes," and now it included "the pride of life" (1 John 2:16). When Samson ate the honey from the lion's carcass, he was defiled by a dead body; and that part of his Nazirite dedication was destroyed. In fact, two thirds of his vow was now gone; for he had defiled himself by going into the vineyard[7] and by eating food from a dead body.

He lost control of his tongue (vv. 10-18). Since Samson hadn't brought any men with him to serve as "friends of the bridegroom" (Matt. 9:15, NKJV), the Philistines rounded up thirty men to do the job for him. These men may also have served as guards for the Philistines; for Samson's reputation had preceded him, and they were never sure what he would do next. Since the atmosphere must have been tense at the beginning of the feast, Samson sought to liven things up by posing a riddle. Sad to say, he constructed the riddle out of the experience of his sin! He didn't take seriously the fact that he had violated his Nazirite vows. It's bad enough to disobey God, but when you make a joke out of it, you've sunk to new depths of spiritual insensitivity.

It would have been an expensive thing for the thirty guests to supply Samson with sixty garments, so they were desperate to learn the answer to the riddle. Their only recourse was to enlist the help of Samson's wife. Thus they threatened to kill her and burn down her father's house if she didn't supply the answer before the week was up. Samson resolutely refused to tell her; but on the seventh day, he relented. Since the marriage was to be consummated on the seventh day, perhaps that had something to do with it. First the Philistine woman enticed him (Jud. 14:1), then she controlled him (v. 17), and then she betrayed him (v. 17), which is the way the world always treats the compromising believer. Samson could kill lions and break ropes, but he couldn't overcome the power of a woman's tears.

We wonder how his wife felt being compared to a heifer? The proverb simply means, "You couldn't have done what you did if you hadn't broken the rules," because heifers weren't used for plowing. Since the guests had played foul, technically Samson could have refused to pay the prize; but he generously agreed to keep his promise. Perhaps he found out that his wife's life had been threatened and he didn't want to put her and her family into jeopardy again.

Those who can't control their tongue can't control their bodies (James 3:2); and in Samson's case, the consequences of this lack of discipline were disastrous.

Samson lost his temper (vv. 19-20). He went twenty miles away to Ashkelon so the news of the slaughter wouldn't get back to Timnah too soon. His joke about the lion and the honey ceased to be a joke, for it led to the death of thirty men whose garments Samson confiscated. Samson was so angry that he didn't even consummate the marriage but went back to Zorah and stayed with his parents.[8] While he was away from Timnah, his wife was given to his best man. The Lord used this turn of events to motivate Samson to decide to fight the Philistines instead of entertaining them.

If Samson had won his way and married a Philistine woman, that relationship would have crippled the work God had called him to do. Believers today who enter into unholy alliances are sinning and hindering the work of the Lord too (2 Cor. 6:14-18). If Samson had sought God's leading, the Lord would have directed him. Instead, Samson went his own way, and the Lord had to overrule his selfish decisions.

"I will instruct you and teach you in the way you should go; I will guide you with My eye. Do not be like the horse or like the mule, which have no understanding, which must be harnessed with bit and bridle, else they will not come near you" (Ps. 32:8-9, NKJV). If we're looking by faith into the face of the Lord, He can guide us with His eye, the way parents guide their children. But if we turn our backs on Him, he has to treat us like animals and harness us. Samson was either impetuously rushing ahead like the horse or stubbornly holding back like the mule, and God had to deal with him.

The Light That Failed

The life of Samson illustrates the ancient truth that a good beginning doesn't guarantee a good ending.[1] The American poet Henry Wadsworth Longfellow said, "Great is the art of beginning, but greater is the art of ending." That's why Solomon wrote, "The end of a matter is better than its beginning" (Ecc. 7:8, NIV).

At the beginning of his career, Samson served in a blaze of glory, but the light began to flicker as he yielded to his passions. In the closing scenes of his life, we watch Samson's light finally go out; and the blind champion ends up buried in the rubble of a heathen temple. Granted, he killed more in his martyrdom than he killed during his judgeship; but how different it would have been had he first conquered himself before he sought to conquer the Lord's enemies. "His whole life," said Spurgeon, "is a series of miracles and follies."

Let's look at the closing scenes in Samson's life and learn from them why he didn't end well.

1. Samson avenges himself (Jud. 15:1-8)

The passion to get even seemed to govern Samson's life. His motto was, "As they did unto me, so have I done unto them"

(15:11). I realize that as the defender of Israel, Samson's calling was to defeat the enemy; but you long to see him fighting "the battles of the Lord" and not just his own private wars. When David faced the Philistines, he saw them as the enemies of the Lord and sought to honor the name of the Lord in his victory (1 Sam. 17). Samson's attitude was different.

As Christians, we need to beware of hiding selfish motives under the cloak of religious zeal and calling it "righteous indignation." Personal vengeance and private gain rather than the glory of the Lord has motivated more than one "crusader" in the church. What some people think is godly zeal may actually be ungodly anger, fed by pride and motivated by selfishness. There is a godly anger that we should experience when we see wickedness prosper and defenseless people hurt (Eph. 4:26), but there's a very fine line between righteous indignation and a "religious temper tantrum."

He avenges his ruined marriage (vv. 1-5). Although he had never consummated the marriage, Samson thought he was legally married to the woman of Timnah. Therefore, he took a gift and went to visit her in her father's house. How shocked he was to learn that not only was he not married, but also the woman he loved was now married to his best-man![2] Samson had paid the legal "bride price" for his wife, and now he had neither the money nor the wife.

Samson was angry, and even the offer of a younger and prettier bride didn't appease him. If anybody should have been punished, it was his father-in-law. He was the real culprit. After all, he took the money and gave the bride away— to the wrong man! But Samson decided to take out his anger on the Philistines by burning up the grain in their fields.

The word translated "foxes" also means "jackals," and that's probably the animal that Samson used. Foxes are solitary creatures, but jackals prowl in large packs. Because of this, it would have been much easier for Samson to capture 300 jackals; and no doubt he enlisted the help of others. Had he tied the firebrands to individual animals, they each would have immediately run to their dens. But by putting two animals together and turning them loose, Samson could be fairly sure that their fear of the fire and their inability to maneuver easily would make them panic. Thus they would run around frantically in the fields and ignite the grain. The fire then would spread into the vineyards and olive groves. It was a costly devastation.

Why he chose to destroy the Philistine's crops in such a strange manner isn't clear to us. If others were helping him, Samson could attack several fields at the same time; and the Philistines, unable to see the animals on the ground, would be alarmed and confused, wondering what was causing the fires. The jackals would undoubtedly make a racket, especially if caught in the rushing flame or overwhelmed by the smoke. His riddle and his rhyme (15:16) indicate that Samson had a boyish sense of humor, and perhaps this approach to agricultural arson was just another fun time for him. However, we must keep in mind that God was using Samson's exploits to harass the Philistines and prepare them for the sure defeat that was coming in a few years.

He avenges his wife's death (vv. 6-8). Violence breeds violence, and the Philistines weren't about to stand around doing nothing while their food and fortune went up in flames. They figured out that Samson was behind the burning of their crops, and they knew they had to retaliate. Since they couldn't hope to overcome Samson, they did the next thing and vented their wrath on his wife and father-in-law. In the long run, her betrayal of Samson didn't save her life after all (14:15).

Samson's response? "Since you've acted like this, I won't stop until I get my revenge on you" (15:7, NIV). We don't know how many Philistines he killed or what weapons he used, but it was "a great slaughter." Following the attack, he retreated to a cave in the "rock of Etam." This is not the Etam mentioned either in 1 Chronicles 4:32 (too far away) or 2 Chronicles 11:6 (hadn't been built yet). It was some elevated place in Judah, near Lehi, from which Samson could safely and conveniently watch the enemy.

2. Samson defends himself (Jud. 15:9-20)

If Samson could attack the Philistines, then the Philistines could retaliate and attack Israel; after all, Israel had neither weapons nor an army. The invasion of Judah didn't help Samson's popularity with his own people, who sadly were content to submit to their neighbors and make the best of a bad situation. Instead of seeing Samson as their deliverer, the men of Judah considered him a troublemaker.

It's difficult to be a leader if you have no followers, but part of the fault lay with Samson. He didn't challenge the people, organize them, and trust God to give them victory. He preferred to work alone, fighting the battles of the Lord as though they were his own private feuds. I realize that Samson's calling was to *begin* to deliver the nation (13:5), but it seems to me that he could have made a more forceful beginning. When God's people get comfortable with the status quo, and their leaders fail to arouse them to action, they are in pretty bad shape.

When the men of Judah learned that the Philistines wanted only to capture and bind Samson, they offered to help. A nation is in a sad state indeed when the citizens cooperate with the enemy and hand over their own God-appointed leader! This is the only time during Samson's judgeship that the Jews mustered an army, *and it was for the purpose of capturing one of their own men!* But Samson realized that, if he didn't give himself up to the enemy, the Philistine army would bring untold suffering to the land; so he willingly surrendered. If he defended himself, he would have had to fight his own people. If he escaped, which he could easily have done, he would have left 3,000 men of Judah easy prey for the Philistine army. There was something heroic about Samson's decision, but the men of Judah missed it.

By the power of the Holy Spirit, Samson easily broke the bonds the men of Judah had put on his arms, picked up a new jawbone of a donkey (an old one would have been too brittle), and slaughtered a thousand Philistines. We wonder what the men of Judah thought as they watched their prisoner, their own brother, kill the invaders single-handed. Did any of them feel the urge to pick up the weapons of the slain Philistines and join in the battle? Would they have known how to use them?

Samson had a way with words. At his wedding feast, he devised a clever riddle (14:14); and after this great victory, he wrote a poem. It's based on the similarity between the sounds of the Hebrew words *hamor* ("donkey") and *homer* ("heap"). James Moffatt renders it: "With the jawbone of an ass I have piled them in a mass. With the jawbone of an ass I have assailed assailants."[3]

But his victory celebration didn't last very long, for God reminded him that he was only a man and had to have water to stay alive. So often in Scripture, testing follows triumph. No sooner had the Israelites crossed the Red Sea than they became thirsty (Ex. 15:22-27) and hungry (Ex. 16). Elijah's victory on Mount Carmel was followed by his humiliating flight to Mount Horeb (1 Kings 18–19). If triumphs aren't balanced with trials, there's a danger that we'll become proud and self-confident.

If Samson had only heeded this warning and asked God not only for water but for guidance! "Lead us not into temptation" would have been the perfect prayer for that hour. How quick we are to cry out for help for the body when perhaps our greatest needs are in the inner person. It's when we're weak that we're strong (2 Cor. 12:10); and when we're totally dependent on the Lord, we're the safest.

Samson's prayer indicates that he considered himself God's servant and that he didn't want to end his life falling into the hands of the godless Philistines. Unfortunately, that's just what happened. But God was merciful and performed a miracle by opening up a spring of water in a hollow place. Samson quenched his thirst and then gave the place the name "Caller's Spring." The place where Samson slaughtered the Philistines received the name "Jawbone Hill." Some translations give the impression that the water came from the jawbone because the name of the place in Hebrew is Lehi, which means "jawbone." In the NKJV, Judges 15:19 reads, "So God split the hollow place that is in Lehi"; and the NASB and NIV are substantially the same.

3. Samson tempts himself (Jud. 16:1-3)

Gaza was an important seaport town located about forty miles from Samson's hometown of Zorah. We aren't told why Samson went there, but it's not likely he was looking for sensual pleasure. There were plenty of prostitutes available in Israel even though the Law condemned this practice (Lev. 19:29; Deut. 22:21). It was after he arrived in Gaza that Samson saw a prostitute and decided to visit her. Once again the lust of the eyes and the lust of the flesh combined to grip Samson and make him a slave to his passions.

It seems incredible to us that a servant of God (Jud. 15:18), who did great works in the power of the Spirit, would visit a prostitute, but the record is here for all to read. The Lord certainly didn't approve of such behavior, especially on the part of a Nazirite; and the experience was for Samson one more step down into darkness and destruction. In recent years, there have been enough ministerial scandals in the United States alone to put all of us on guard. "Therefore let him who thinks he stands take heed lest he fall" (1 Cor. 10:12, NKJV).

We can't help it when Satan and his demons tempt us; but when we tempt ourselves, we become our own enemy. God doesn't tempt us (James 1:12-15). When we pray, "Lead us not into temptation" (Matt. 6:13), we're asking that we not tempt ourselves *or put ourselves into such a position that we tempt God.* We tempt Him either by forcing Him to intervene and rescue us or by daring Him to stop us. It's possible for people's character to deteriorate so much that they don't have to be tempted in order to sin. All they need is the opportunity to sin, and they'll tempt themselves. Illicit sexual experience may begin as sweet as honey, but it ends up as bitter as wormwood (Prov. 5:1-14). Samson the man had become Samson the animal as the prostitute led him to the slaughter (Prov. 7:6-23).

Word that their enemy Samson was in town spread to the people of Gaza, and they posted a guard at the city gate to capture him and kill him in the morning. But Samson decided to leave town at midnight, while the guards were asleep. The fact that the city gates were barred didn't alarm him. He picked up the doors, posts, and bars and carried them off! Whether he carried them all the way to Hebron, a distance of about forty miles, or only to a hill that faced Hebron, depends on how you translate Judges 16:3. Both interpretations are possible.

The city gate was not only a protection for the city, but also the place where the officials met to transact business (Deut. 25:7; Ruth 4:1-2). To "possess the gate of his enemies" was a metaphor meaning "to defeat your enemies" (Gen. 22:17; 24:60). When Jesus spoke about the gates of hell (hades) not prevailing against the church (Matt. 16:18), He was picturing the victory of the church over the forces of Satan and evil. Through His death and resurrection, Jesus Christ has "stormed the gates of hell" and carried them off in victory!

4. Samson betrays himself (Jud. 16:4-22)

The Valley of Sorek lay between Zorah and Timnah on the border of Judah and Philistia. The city of Beth-shemesh was located there. Whenever Samson went into enemy territory, he "went down" both geographically and spiritually (14:1, 5, 7, 10). This time he found a woman in the valley, not too far from home; and he fell in love with her. It's a dangerous thing to linger at the enemy's border; you might get caught.

Along with David and Bathsheba, Samson and Delilah have captured the imagination of scores of writers, artists, composers, and dramatists. Handel included Delilah in his oratorio "Samson," and Saint-Saens wrote an opera on "Samson and Delilah." (The "Bacchanale" from that work is still a popular concert piece.) When Samson consorted with Delilah in the Valley of Sorek, he never dreamed that what they did together would be made into a Hollywood movie and projected in color on huge screens.

Scholars disagree on the meaning of Delilah's name. Some think it means "devotee," suggesting that she may have been a temple prostitute. But Delilah isn't called a prostitute as is the woman in Gaza, although that's probably what she was. For that matter, Delilah isn't even identified as a Philistine. However, from her dealings with the Philistine leaders, she appears to be one. Other students believe that the basis for her name is the Hebrew word *dalal*, which means "to weaken, to impoverish." Whether or not this is the correct derivation, she certainly weakened and impoverished Samson!

Each of the Philistine leaders offered to pay Delilah a considerable sum of money if she would entice Samson and learn the source of his great strength.[4] They didn't want to kill Samson. They wanted to neutralize his power, capture him, torture him, and then use him for their own purposes. Being able to exhibit and control the great champion of Israel would give the Philistines both security and stature among the nations and would certainly satisfy their egos as they humiliated the Jews.

When Delilah began to probe for the secret of his strength, Samson should have been aware of his danger and, like Joseph (Gen. 39:12; 2 Tim. 2:22), fled as fast as possible. But passion had gripped him, sin had anesthetized him, and he was unable to act rationally. Anybody could have told him that Delilah was making a fool out of him, but Samson would have believed no one.

It's unlikely that the Philistines who hid in her chamber revealed themselves each time Samson escaped his bonds, because then he would have known that Delilah had set a trap for him. Her cry "The Philistines are upon you!" was the signal for the spies to be alert; but when they saw that Samson was free, they remained in hiding. Each of Samson's lies involved Delilah using some kind of bonds on him, but the Philistines should have known that he could not be bound (Jud. 15:13).

Delilah had to keep working on Samson or she would have lost the money and perhaps her life. After all, look at what the Philistines did to Samson's first wife! If Samson had stopped visiting Delilah, he would have kept his hair and his power,[5] but he kept going back, and each time she implored him to reveal his secret. Samson didn't know his own heart. He thought he possessed enough moral strength to say no to the temptress, but he was wrong.

Being wise in the ways of sin (Luke 16:8; Prov. 7:21), during the fourth visit, Delilah knew that he had finally told her the truth. Since the Philistine "hit squad" had quit coming after the third fiasco, Delilah summoned them quickly, and they once again hid in her chamber.

When Delilah's shout awakened Samson, he thought it was another one of her tricks and that he could handle the situation as before. But he was wrong. When he lost his long hair, the Lord left him; and he was as weak as other men. His power was from the Lord, not from his hair; but the hair was the sign of his Nazirite vow. The Spirit who had come upon him with such power had now departed from him.

Numbers 6:7 reads literally "because the consecration (nezer) of his God is upon his head." The basic meaning of the word nezer is "separation" or "consecration"; but it is also used of a royal crown (2 Sam. 1:10; Zech. 9:16; Ps. 89:39). Samson's long hair was his "royal crown" and he lost it because of his sin. "Behold, I come quickly! Hold fast what you have, that no one may take your crown" (Rev. 3:11, NKJV). Since Samson didn't discipline his body, he lost both his crown and his prize (1 Cor. 9:24-27).[6]

The Philistines easily overpowered Samson and finally had their way with him. They put out his eyes,[7] bound him, and took him to Gaza where he toiled at the grinding mill, doing work usually assigned to slaves, women, or donkeys. Someone has said that Judges 16:21 reminds us of the *blinding, binding,* and *grinding* results of sin. In his epic poem *Samson Agonistes,* John Milton has the champion say:

O loss of sight, of thee I most complain!
Blind among enemies, O worse than chains,
Dungeon, or beggary, or decrepit age!

Samson is one of three men in Scripture who are especially identified with the darkness. The other two are King Saul, who went out in the darkness to get last-minute help from a witch (1 Sam. 28), and Judas, who "went immediately out:

and it was night" (John 13:30). Saul lived for the world, Samson yielded to the flesh, and Judas gave himself to the devil (John 13:2, 27); and all three ended up taking their own lives.

But there was one ray of light in the darkness: Samson's hair began to grow again. His power was not in his hair but in what his hair symbolized—his dedication to God. If Samson renewed that dedication, God might restore his power. I believe Samson talked to the Lord as he turned the millstone, confessing his sins and asking God for one last opportunity to defeat the enemy and glorify His name.[8]

5. Samson destroys himself (Jud. 16:23-31)

It was tragic that a servant of the Lord, raised in a godly home, was now the humiliated slave of the enemy. But even worse, the Philistines gave glory to their god Dagon for helping them capture their great enemy. Instead of bringing glory to the God of Israel, Samson gave the enemy opportunity to honor their false gods. Dagon was the god of grain, and certainly the Philistines remembered what Samson had done to their fields (15:1-5).

The people at the religious festival called for Samson to be brought to entertain them. They were in high spirits because their enemy was now in their control and Dagon had triumphed over Jehovah. They thought that Samson's blindness rendered him harmless. They didn't know that God had deigned to forgive him and restore his strength.

In the KJV, two different words are translated "make sport" in 16:25 ("entertain" and "perform" in the NIV). The first means to celebrate, frolic, joke, and entertain; and the second means to perform, make sport, and laugh.[9] We aren't told exactly *how* Samson entertained the huge crowd in Dagon's temple, but one thing is sure: He gave them every reason to believe he was harmless and under their control. He was even in the hands of a boy who was leading the blind man from place to place. We've seen previous indications that Samson was a clever fellow with a sense of humor. Thus no doubt he gave the audience just what it wanted.

In previous visits to Gaza, Samson had undoubtedly seen this temple and noted its construction. After all, it housed over 3,000 people, and it would be difficult for him not to notice it. During a break in the day's entertainment, Samson asked his attendant to lead him over to the pillars; and there he uttered his last prayer.[10] The fact that God answered suggests that all was right between him and his Lord (Ps. 66:18-19).

It's likely that his parents were dead by now, but his relatives on his father's side came and recovered the body and buried it. The word "brethren" in Judges 16:31 in the Hebrew carries a broad meaning of "relatives." As far as we know, Samson was an only child. The phrase "between Zorah and Eshtaol" in verse 31 reminds us of 13:25. Samson is back where he started, only now he's dead. The light has failed.

How do you assess the life and ministry of a man like Samson? I think Alexander Maclaren says it well: "Instead of trying to make a lofty hero out of him, it is far better to recognize frankly the limitations of his character and the imperfections of his religion. . . . If the merely human passion of vengeance throbbed fiercely in Samson's prayer, he had never heard 'Love your enemies'; and, for his epoch, the destruction of the enemies of God and of Israel was duty."[11]

His decline began when he disagreed with his parents about marrying a Philistine girl. Then he disdained his Nazirite vow and defiled himself. He disregarded the warnings of God, disobeyed the Word of God, and was defeated by the enemies of God. He probably thought that he had the privilege of indulging in sin since he wore the badge of a Nazirite and won so many victories for the Lord, but he was wrong.

"Whoever has no rule over his own spirit is like a city broken down, without walls" (Prov. 25:28, NKJV).

"He who is slow to anger is better than the mighty, and he who rules his spirit than he who takes a city" (Prov. 16:32, NKJV).

I wonder whether Solomon was thinking about Samson when he wrote those words.

"The Center Cannot Hold"

In his well-known poem "The Second Coming," the Irish poet William Butler Yeats describes the collapse of civilization in vivid and frightening imagery. Each time I read the poem, I feel chilled within; and then I give thanks that I know the One who is coming.

"Things fall apart," writes Yeats; "the center cannot hold."

The closing chapters of the Book of Judges echo that theme: "the center cannot hold." The nation that once marched triumphantly through Canaan to the glory of God now disintegrates morally and politically and brings disgrace to His name. But what else can you expect when there is "no king in Israel" and the people are flouting the laws of God?

The events described in chapters 17–21 took place earlier in the period of the Judges, probably before the forty-year rule of the Philistines. The movements of the tribe of Dan would have been difficult and the war against Benjamin impossible if the Philistines had been in charge at that time. The writer departed from historical chronology and put these events together as an "appendix" to the book to show how wicked the people had become. In three major areas of life, things were falling apart: the home, the ministry, and society.

1. Confusion in the home (Jud. 17:1-6)

God has established three institutions in society: the home, human government, and the worshiping community—Israel under the Old Covenant and the church under the New Covenant. The first of these, in both time and significance, is the home, because the home is the basis for society. When God wedded Adam to Eve in the garden, He laid the foundation for the social institutions humanity would build. When that foundation crumbles, society begins to fall apart. "If the foundations be destroyed, what can the righteous do?" (Ps. 11:3)

The name Micah means "Who is like Jehovah?" but the man certainly didn't live to honor the Lord. He had a family (Jud. 17:5), although nothing is said about his wife; and we get the impression that his mother lived with him and that she was wealthy. The "extended family" was normal in Israel.

Somebody stole 1,100 shekels of silver from Grandmother, and she pronounced a curse on the thief, not knowing that she was cursing her own son. It was the fear of the curse, not the fear of the Lord, that motivated the son to confess his crime and restore the money. Then Grandmother joyfully neutralized the curse by blessing her son. In gratitude for the return of her money, she dedicated part of the silver to the Lord and made an idol out of it. Her son added the new idol to his "god collection" in his house, a "shrine" cared for by one of his sons whom Micah had consecrated as priest.

Have you ever seen a family more spiritually and morally confused than this one? They managed to break almost all the Ten Commandments (Ex. 20:1-17) *and yet not feel the least bit guilty before the Lord!* In fact, they thought they were serving the Lord by the bizarre things they did!

The son didn't honor his mother; instead, he stole from her and then lied about it. First, he coveted the silver, and then he took it. (According to Col. 3:5, covetousness is idolatry.)

Then he lied about the whole enterprise until the curse scared him into confessing. Thus he broke the fifth, eighth, ninth, and tenth commandments; and he broke the first and second commandments by having a shrine of false gods in his home. According to Proverbs 30:8-9, when he stole the silver, he broke the third commandment and took the name of the Lord in vain. Breaking seven of the Ten Commandments without leaving your own home is quite an achievement!

The man's mother broke the first two commandments by making an idol and encouraging her son to maintain a private "shrine" in his home. According to Deuteronomy 12:1-14, there was to be but one place of worship in Israel; and the people were not permitted to have their own private shrines. Furthermore, Micah's mother didn't really deal with her son's sins; his character certainly didn't improve by the way she handled the matter. But she was a corrupt person herself, so what else could he expect?

Micah not only had a private shrine, but also he ordained his own son to serve as priest. Certainly Micah knew that the Lord had appointed the family of Aaron to be the only priests in Israel; and if anybody outside Aaron's family served as priests, they were to be killed (Num. 3:10).

Because Micah and his family didn't submit to the authority of God's Word, their home was a place of religious and moral confusion. But their home was a good deal like many homes today where money is the god the family worships, where children steal from their parents and lie about what they do, where family honor is unknown, and where the true God is unwanted. Television provides all the "images" the family will ever want to "worship," and few worry about "thus saith the Lord."

I recall hearing Vance Havner say, "We shouldn't worry because the government won't allow children to have Bibles in school. They'll get free Bibles when they go to prison."

But today our prisons are so crowded that the government doesn't know what to do. If every family would make Christ the Head of the home, we could stop some of the nation's crime right at the source. Godly homes are the foundation for a just and happy society.

2. Confusion in the ministry (Jud. 17:7-13)

Not only did God establish the home and instruct parents how to raise their children (Deut. 6), but also He instituted spiritual leadership in the worshiping community. Under the Old Covenant, the tabernacle and then the temple were the center of the community, and the Aaronic priesthood supervised both. Under the New Covenant, the church of Jesus Christ is the temple of God (Eph. 2:19-22); and the Holy Spirit calls and equips ministers to serve Him and His people (1 Cor. 12–14; Eph. 4:1-16). In His Word, God told the Old Testament priests what they were supposed to do; and in His Word today, the Holy Spirit guides His church and explains its order and its ministry.

A young Levite named Jonathan (18:30)[1] had been living in Bethlehem of Judah, which was not one of the cities assigned to the priests and Levites (Josh. 21; Num. 35). He was probably there because the people of Israel weren't supporting the tabernacle and its ministry with their tithes and offerings as God commanded them to do (Num. 18:21-32; Deut. 14:28-29; 26:12-15). Why live in one of the levitical cities if you're going to starve? When God's people grow indifferent to spiritual things, one of the first evidences of their apathy is a decline in their giving to the work of the Lord; as a result, everybody suffers.

Instead of seeking the mind of the Lord, Jonathan set out to find a place to live and work, even if it meant abandoning his calling as a servant of God. The nation was at a low ebb spiritually and he could have done something to help bring the people back to God. He was only one man, but that's all God needs to begin a great work that can make a difference in the history of a nation. Instead of being available to God, Jonathan was agreeable only to men; and he eventually found himself a comfortable home and job with Micah.

If Jonathan is typical of God's servants in that period of history, then it's no wonder the nation of Israel was confused and corrupt. He had no appreciation for his high calling as a Levite, a chosen servant of God. Not only were the Levites to assist the priests in their ministries (Num. 3:6-13; 8:17-18), but also they were to teach the Law to the people (Neh. 8:7-9; 2 Chron. 17:7-9; 35:3) and be involved in the sacred music and the praises of Israel (1 Chron. 23:28-32; Ezra 3:10). Jonathan gave all that up for comfort and security in the home of an idolater.

Jonathan's ministry, however, wasn't a spiritual ministry at all. To begin with, he was *a hireling* and not a true shepherd (Jud. 18:4; John 10:12-13). He didn't serve the true and living God; he worked for Micah and his idols. Jonathan wasn't a spokesperson for the Lord; he gave people just the message they wanted to hear (Jud. 18:6). When he was offered a place involving more money, more people, and more prestige, he took it immediately and gave thanks for it (v. 19). And then he assisted his new employers in stealing his former employer's gods!

Whenever the church has a "hireling ministry," it can't enjoy the blessing of God. The church needs true and faithful shepherds who work for the Lord, not for personal gain, and who will stay with the flock to feed them and protect them. True shepherds don't see their work as a "career" and run off to a "better job" when the opportunity comes. They stay where God puts them and don't move until He sends them.

True shepherds receive their calling and authority from God, not from people (Gal. 1:6ff); and they honor the true

God, not the idols that people make. It must grieve the Lord today to see people worshiping the idols of ministerial "success," statistics, buildings, and reputation. In today's "consumer society," self-appointed preachers and "prophets" have no problem getting a following and peddling their religious wares to a church that acts more like a Hollywood fan club than a holy people of God. And to make it worse, these hirelings will call what's happening "the blessing of God." Jonathans and Micahs will always find each other because they need each other.

The sad part of the story is that Micah now thought he had the favor of God because a genuine levitical priest was serving as his private chaplain. Micah practiced a false religion and worshiped false gods (with Jehovah thrown in for good measure), and all the while he rested on the false confidence that God was blessing him! Little did he know that the day would come when his priest and his gods would be taken from him and nothing would be left of his religion.

3. Confusion in society (Jud. 18:1-31)

God should have been the king in Israel and His Word the law that governed society, but the people preferred to "do their own thing." If the people had forsaken their idols, and if the elders of Israel had consulted God's Law and obeyed it for God's glory, Israel could have been governed successfully. Instead, "Every man did that which was right in his own eyes" (21:25), and the result was a society filled with competition and confusion.

Consider the sins of the tribe of Dan as they sought to better their situation in the nation of Israel.

Covetousness (vv. 1-2). The tribe of Dan descended from Jacob's fifth son, born of Rachel's handmaid Bilhah (Gen. 30:1-6). Though not a large tribe (Num. 1:39), it was given choice territory when the tribal boundaries were assigned

(Josh. 19:40-48). The Danites, however, weren't able to defeat and dispossess the enemy (Jud. 1:34), thus they decided to go north and relocate. Most of the other tribes were able to conquer the enemy, dispossessed them, and claim their land, but the Danites coveted somebody else's land instead and took it in a violent manner.

The Lord had assigned the tribal allotments under the direction of Joshua, with the help of Eleazar the high priest and the elders from the tribes (Josh. 19:51). As He did with the nations (Acts 17:26), so He did with the tribes: God put each tribe just where He wanted it. For the tribe of Dan to reject God's assigned territory and covet another place was to oppose His divine will.

But isn't that what causes most of the trouble in our society today? Instead of submitting to God's will, people want what somebody else has; and they'll do almost anything to get it (James 4:1-3). The corruption that's in this world is fed by "evil desires" (2 Peter 1:4, NIV). Whether it's producing pornography, selling dope, or promoting gambling, money-hungry people cater to human desires and end up making money and destroying lives. Thanks to the power of modern media, especially television, the advertising industry creates in people appetites for all sorts of exciting products, services, and experiences. Therefore, people go out and spend money they don't have on things they don't need to impress people who don't really care; but this is the cycle that keeps business going.[2]

The elders of Israel should have put a stop to the men of Dan as they abandoned God's assigned place and headed north to kill innocent people and steal their land. But covetousness is strong; and once people get an appetite for "something more," it's difficult to control them.

Ungodly counsel (vv. 3-6). It was Jonathan's dialect that attracted the attention of the five spies, because he didn't speak quite like a man from Ephraim. When they asked what a levitical priest was doing in a private home in Ephraim—a very good question, by the way (1 Kings 19:9, 13)—he told them the truth: He was hired to do the job! Since somebody else was paying the bill, the spies thought it was permissible to get "spiritual counsel" from Jonathan, and he told them what they wanted to hear.[3]

If the tribe of Dan had really wanted God's counsel, they could have consulted with the high priest. But they were actually rejecting God's counsel by refusing to remain in the land He had assigned to them. Therefore, it wasn't likely God would have revealed anything to them (John 7:17).

Breaking and entering, robbery and intimidation (vv. 14-26). On their way to capture Laish, the people of Dan paused at Micah's house in Ephraim. The spies told the men that Micah had a wonderful collection of gods, hinting, of course, that the collection would be valuable to them as they traveled, warred, and established their new home. While the armed men stood at the gate of the city, the five spies, who knew Jonathan, invaded the shrine and stole the gods.

When the five men, with their religious loot, arrived back at the city gate, the priest was shocked to see what they had done.[4] But the Danites silenced him by hiring him; and since he was a hireling, Jonathan was ready for a better offer. The Danites not only broke into Micah's shrine and stole his gods, but they also stole his chaplain. Not a bad day's work!

The Danites put the women and children in the front since that was the safest place, because any attacks would come from the rear. By the time the Danites had traveled some distance away, Micah discovered that his shrine was out of business, having neither gods nor priest; so he called his neighbors together, and they pursued the invaders. After all, a man must protect his gods!

It was useless. Since the Danites outnumbered him and

were too strong for him, Micah and his neighbors had to turn around and go home defeated. Micah's sad question "What else do I have?" (v. 24, NIV) reveals the folly and the tragedy of religion without the true and living God. Idolaters worship gods they can carry, but Christians worship a God who carries them (Isa. 46:1-7).

Violence and murder (vv. 7-13, 27-29). The five spies had traveled 100 miles north from their encampment at Zorah to Laish ("Leshem," Josh. 19:47), a town inhabited by the Sidonians, about thirty miles east of the Mediterranean Sea. These were a peaceful people who minded their own business and had no treaties with anybody. They were "unsuspecting and secure" and "prosperous" (v. 7, NIV), an isolated people, who were a perfect target for the warlike tribe of Dan.

With 600 armed men, plus their women and children (Jud. 18:21), they marched north and captured Laish, killing all the inhabitants and burning the city. Then they rebuilt it and proudly called it Dan, after the name of the founder of their tribe. Unfortunately, what Jacob prophesied about the tribe of Dan came true (Gen. 49:17).

Someone has said that there are only three philosophies of life in today's world: (1) "What's mine is mine, I'll keep it"; (2) "What's yours is mine, I'll take it"; and (3) "What's mine is yours, I'll share it." The Danites followed the second philosophy, and so do too many other grasping people. One of the current booming industries in the United States is the installing of security systems in private homes. The number of shooting sprees in shopping malls and fast-food restaurants has frightened many people into doing their shopping by telephone. The cover story of *Time* magazine for August 23, 1993 called the United States "America the Violent."[5]

We don't know how many people lived in Laish, but the wanton murders of even a few hundred innocent people is a crime of gross proportions. I fear that we've been exposed to so much crime and violence in the media that this kind of news doesn't disturb us anymore. "We're seeing a new sort of violence," wrote Arthur Beisser in *Sports Illustrated* (March 1, 1976). "It's being used not as a means to an end, but for recreational purposes, for pleasure." We might add that violence is also a means for making money, as both the moviemakers and the television industry have proved.

Idolatry (vv. 30-31). The tribe of Dan was the first tribe in Israel to officially adopt an idolatrous system of religion. Even though there was a house of God in Shiloh, they preferred their images and idols. Years later, when the kingdom divided, Jeroboam I of Israel would set up golden calves in Dan and Beersheba and encourage the whole nation to turn away from the true and living God (1 Kings 12:25-33).[6]

The account of Micah, Jonathan, and the Danites is more than a story from ancient history. It's a revelation of the wickedness of the human heart and the hopelessness of human society without God. Our modern world has substituted idols for the true and living God and has devised its own humanistic religion, complete with "priests"—the experts who tell us that the Bible is wrong but their way is right. But neither their idols nor their priests have any power against the violence of the human heart.

When Dwight D. Eisenhower was President of the United States, he called a "White House Conference on Children and Youth," hoping to find solutions to the juvenile delinquency problem that was then plaguing the nation. I was supposed to attend that conference but couldn't go because of family obligations.

However, a friend of mine from Youth for Christ International attended and gave this report (I paraphrase): "I sat in the room for hours, listening to psychologists and educators and criminologists talk about teenagers and how to help them, and I got sick of it. Finally, I asked for the floor and told them of our experiences in Youth for Christ, how delinquents had been changed by the power of the Gospel. The room became very quiet, and then people got embarrassed and began to clear their throats and shuffle papers. The chairman thanked me for my words and immediately moved to the next item on the agenda. Then it hit me: *they didn't want to hear!*"

William Butler Yeats was right: "The center cannot hold." The home, the ministry, and society are disintegrating before our eyes, *and people don't want to hear the truth!* But whether they want it or not, the world must be told that Jesus Christ died for lost sinners, and that the power of Christ can transform hearts, homes, churches, and society if people will only trust Him.

"Christ beats His drum, but He does not press men," said English preacher and poet John Donne (d. 1631); "Christ is served with voluntaries."

Are you available?

TWELVE

War and Peace

After reading these three chapters, if you were to scan your daily newspaper or weekly news magazine, you'd have to admit that times haven't changed too much. For in these closing pages of Judges you find reports of wife abuse, blatant homosexuality, gang rape leading to murder, injustice, brother killing brother, and even kidnapping. It's the kind of narrative that almost makes you agree with British essayist Samuel Johnson, who said back in 1783, "I have lived to see things all as bad as they can be." What would he say today?

Of course, events like these are the daily food of people who enjoy TV violence; and researchers tell us that what happens on the screens is often duplicated on the streets. According to a study by the American Psychological Association, there are five violent acts per hour in prime-time TV programs; and on Saturday mornings when the children watch cartoons, violent acts per hour multiply five times (*USA Today*, August 2, 1993). When a nation is entertained by violence, is there much hope for that nation?

When evil isn't dealt with properly, it has a tendency to grow. Sin in the city of Gibeah eventually infected the tribe of Benjamin and led to war in the land of Israel.

1. The wickedness of a city (Jud. 19:1-28)

Entertainment in Bethlehem (vv. 1-9). If you thought that the Levite Jonathan (chaps. 17–18) was a reprobate, then you'll probably conclude that this unnamed Levite was an absolute scoundrel of the basest sort. He spent most of his time partying (19:4, 6, 8, 22); he walked in darkness and jeopardized his life and the lives of those with him (vv. 9-14); he treated his concubine in the most shocking manner, while she was alive and after she was dead; and what he did to her precipitated a civil war in Israel.

A concubine was a lawful wife who was guaranteed only food, clothing, and marital privileges (Ex. 21:7-11; Deut. 21:10-14). Any children she bore would be considered legitimate; but because of her second-class status, they wouldn't necessarily share in the family inheritance (Gen. 25:1-6). If a man's wife was barren, he sometimes took a concubine so he could establish a family. Though the law controlled concubinage the Lord did not approve or encourage it; yet you will find several Old Testament men who had concubines, including Abraham, Jacob, Gideon, Saul, David, and Solomon.

This particular concubine was unfaithful to her husband and fled to her father's house in Bethlehem for protection (Lev. 20:10). The longer she was gone, the more her husband missed her; so he traveled to Bethlehem, forgave her, and was reconciled. He and his father-in-law discovered they enjoyed each other's company and spent five days eating, drinking, and making merry. Little did the Levite realize that he really had nothing to be happy about because tragedy was stalking his marriage.

To me, this Levite illustrates the careless attitude of many believers today. They are children of the day, but they act like children of the night (1 Thes. 5:1-8). Judgment is around the corner, but these people think of nothing but enjoying life. When his nation was so far from God, how could this

Levite waste his time eating, drinking, and making merry? "Be afflicted, and mourn, and weep: let your laughter be turned to mourning, and your joy to heaviness" (James 4:9).

Yes, there's "a time to laugh" (Ecc. 3:4), and God wants us to enjoy His gifts (1 Tim. 6:17); but for many Christians, that time is *all the time!* In too many churches, the laughter of "religious entertainment" has replaced the holy hush of worship. The sanctuary has become a theater. When the saints get together, the most important thing is to "have fun." In order to salve our consciences, we have a "short devotional" before the fun time ends; and we piously thank God that we've had such a good time.

Nobody appreciates laughter and good humor more than I do, but I fear the church is losing its sense of awe and needs to learn how to weep. Had this laughing Levite been walking in the light, praying and seeking God's will, he would have made other plans and saved his wife from shame, abuse, pain, and death.

Hospitality in Gibeah (vv. 10-21). During the period of the Judges, it was dangerous to travel in the daytime (5:6) and even more so at night. The Levite didn't want to stay in Jerusalem because it was in the hands of the pagan Jebusites. Thus he pressed on four miles to Gibeah so he could be with his own people. *But the men of Gibeah turned out to be as wicked as the heathen around them!*

To begin with, nobody in Gibeah welcomed the visitors and opened their home to care for them. Since the Levite had plenty of provisions for his party and his animals, he wouldn't have been a burden to anybody; but nobody took them in. Hospitality is one of the sacred laws of the East, and no stranger was to be neglected; but only one man in the city showed any concern, and he was an Ephraimite. He not only took them into his home but also used his own provisions to feed them and their animals.

God's people are commanded to practice hospitality. It's one of the qualifications for a pastor (1 Tim. 3:2; Titus 1:8). "Do not forget to entertain strangers, for by so doing some people have entertained angels without knowing it" (Heb. 13:2, NIV).

Iniquity in Gibeah (vv. 22-28). Gibeah had become like Sodom, a city so wicked that God wiped it off the face of the earth (Gen. 19). The men of the city were indulging in immoral practices that were contrary to nature (Rom. 1:24-27) and the laws of God (Lev. 18:22; 20:13; see 1 Cor. 6:9-10). The word "know" in Judges 19:22 means "to have sexual experience with." These sinners were excited because a new man was in town, and they wanted to enjoy him.

The host courageously and correctly described their desires as wickedness and folly (v. 23) and a vile thing (v. 24), and he tried to prevent them from raping his guest. Like Lot in Sodom, the host offered them his daughter, which shows the low estimate some men in that day had of women and of sexual purity. How a father could offer his own daughter as a sacrifice to the lusts of a mob is difficult to understand. Yet many parents today allow their sons' and daughters' minds and hearts to be violated by what they see and hear in movies, on television, and at rock concerts. Chastity of mind and heart is essential for chastity of the body.

Since the Levite was afraid the mob would kill him (20:5), he pacified them by giving them his concubine; and she had to endure gang rape the whole night (v. 25). Our hearts revolt at the thought of a man so insensitive to the feelings of a human being made in the image of God, so indifferent to the sanctity of sex and the responsibility of marriage, and so unconcerned about the laws of God, that he would sacrifice his wife to save his own skin. Was he punishing her for being unfaithful to him? If so, the punishment was far greater than the sin.

But it gets worse. Not only did the Levite surrender his wife to the perverted appetites of an ungodly mob, but also he was able to *lie down and go to sleep* while they were abusing her in the street! How calloused can a man become? And how naive was he to expect that she would be alive the next morning?

Finding her dead on the doorstep, but not feeling guilty about it, he put her corpse on one of the donkeys and made his way home. Then he did a despicable thing: He desecrated and mutilated her corpse by cutting it into twelve parts and sending one part to each of the twelve tribes of Israel. Of course, he wanted to mobilize the support of the tribes and punish the men of Gibeah who had killed his wife, but in fact, he was the one who had let them kill her! Surely there were other ways to call attention to Gibeah's crime.[1]

Had the Levite gone to Shiloh where the tabernacle stood (18:31), and had he consulted with the high priest, he could have dealt with the matter according to the Law of God and avoided causing a great deal of trouble. Once tempers were heated in Israel, however, it was difficult to stop the fire from spreading.

2. The stubbornness of a tribe (Jud. 20:1-48)

The assembly (vv. 1-11). The Levite's gruesome announcement produced the results that he wanted: Leaders and soldiers from the entire nation, except Benjamin (v. 3) and Jabesh-gilead (21:8-9), came together at Mizpah to determine what to do.[2] After hearing the Levite's indictment of the men of Gibeah, the people of Israel delivered a verdict and made a vow. The verdict was that the men of Gibeah were guilty and should be handed over to the authorities to be slain (Deut. 13:12-18). The vow was that none of the tribes represented would give their daughters in marriage to the men of Benjamin (Jud. 21:1-7).

The appeal (vv. 12-17). The eleven tribes had agreed "as one man" to attack Gibeah, but first they sent representatives throughout the tribe of Benjamin, calling for the people to confess their wickedness and hand over the guilty men. According to Leviticus 20:13, homosexuals were to be put to death; but that wasn't the crime the tribes were judging. Since the Levite had *willingly* given his concubine to the men of Gibeah, their sin can hardly be called adultery (Deut. 22:22). The penalty for rape was death, and gang rape would be even more serious (Deut. 22:25-26). Perhaps the tribes were citing the law concerning wicked men in a city (Deut. 13:12-18) and using that as the basis for their action.

Whatever law they were obeying, the tribes were concerned to "put away evil out of the land," a phrase that is found at least nine times in Deuteronomy. The men of Gibeah were evil men and had to be punished before the Lord could be pleased with His people and cleanse His land. But the people of Benjamin wouldn't admit that Gibeah had sinned, nor would they turn over the men who had done the wicked deed.

Some people may have interpreted the stubbornness of Benjamin as an act of patriotism: They were only trying to protect their own citizens. But their refusal to cooperate was definitely an act of rebellion against the Lord. When sin isn't exposed, confessed, and punished, it pollutes society and defiles the land. The wicked men of Gibeah were like a cancerous tumor in the body that had to be cut out. "Your glorying is not good. Do you not know that a little leaven leavens the whole lump?" (1 Cor. 5:6, NKJV)

The result? The tribe of Benjamin declared war on the rest of the tribes of Israel! The eleven tribes had 400,000 men in their army (Jud. 20:2), while the Benjamites had only 26,000 swordsmen and 700 "chosen men" who were experts with slings (vv. 15-16). But in spite of the terrible odds, *it was brother fighting against brother!*

When God's people refuse to obey God's Word, the results are always tragic. The spiritual life of a church is crippled and eventually destroyed when the congregation shuts its eyes to sin and will not discipline offenders. There can never be unity among the people of God as long as some of them cover up sin and allow it to infect the body.

The attack (vv. 18-40). The representatives of the eleven tribes went to the tabernacle at Shiloh (18:31; 1 Sam. 1:9)[3] and sought the mind of the Lord, either by casting lots (Jud. 20:9) or by the priest using the Urim and Thummim (Ex. 28:30). God gave them permission to do battle, with the tribe of Judah leading the attack. That first day, God allowed the Benjamites to win and kill 22,000 Israelite soldiers.

The eleven tribes wept before the Lord and again sought His will. Note that "the children of Benjamin" in Judges 20:18 becomes "Benjamin my brother" in verse 23. Perhaps this was one reason why God permitted the Israelites to lose that first battle. It gave them an opportunity to reflect on the fact that they were fighting their own flesh and blood. But on the second day of the war, Benjamin won again, this time killing 18,000 men. The situation was very grim.

The eleven tribes again sought the face of the Lord, this time with fasting and sacrifices along with their tears. The Lord answered their prayers and not only told them to attack again but also assured them that this time they would win.

The strategy used on the third day was similar to that which Joshua used at Ai (Josh. 8). Self-confident because of two days of victories (Jud. 20:30-31, and note 16:20), the army of Benjamin met the Israelite army, killed about 30 men, but were drawn away from Gibeah and caught in an ambush. Over 25,000 Benjamites were killed on the battlefield, on the highways, or as they fled into the wilderness. Gibeah was taken, its inhabitants were slain, and the city was burned to the ground. In fact, the Israelite army wiped out several other cities in a mopping-up operation.

At the first census after the exodus from Egypt, there were 35,400 men of war in Benjamin (Num. 1:37), and this increased to 45,600 by the time of the second census (Num. 26:41). During this three-day war, the Benjamites were left with only 600 men stranded on the rock of Rimmon, a fortresslike rock formation near Gibeah. What a price the tribe of Benjamin paid for refusing to obey the Law of the Lord!

3. The brokenness of a nation (Jud. 21:1-25)

Once their anger cooled off, the eleven tribes realized that they had just about eliminated a tribe from the nation of Israel; and this made them weep (vv. 2, 15). They offered sacrifices to the Lord, but there's no record that the people humbled themselves, confessed their sin, and sought the help of the Lord. Previously, the Lord had revealed His will to them (20:18, 23, 28); but there's no evidence that they received His Word after the battle was over.

I may be wrong, but I suspect that the Lord wasn't pleased with the people of Benjamin because they still hadn't confessed their sin and admitted they were wrong. The 600 soldiers who were stranded on the rock of Rimmon still weren't seeking God's face. They were simply fleeing from the victorious army. Had somebody suggested that they all meet the Lord at Shiloh and get the matter settled with the Lord, it might have made a difference.

Instead of getting directions from the Lord, the eleven tribes depended on their own wisdom to solve the problem (James 3:13-18). The 600 men who were left from Benjamin would need wives if they were going to reestablish their tribe, but the eleven tribes had sworn not to give them wives. Where would these wives come from?

The Israelites solved the problem by killing more of their own people! Nobody had come to the war from Jabesh-gilead, which meant two things: They hadn't participated in the oath, and the city deserved to be punished. It's possible that when the twelve parts of the concubine's body were sent throughout Israel, a warning was issued that any tribe or city that didn't respond and help fight Benjamin would be treated the same way. That's the kind of warning King Saul gave when he used a similar approach (1 Sam. 11:7).

If that's the case, then the men of Jabesh-gilead knew what was at stake when they remained at home; and the ensuing slaughter of their city was their own fault. The executioners found 400 virgins in the city, women who could become wives to two thirds of the soldiers on the rock. These men had been on the rock for four months (Jud. 20:47), but now they could take their brides and go home. What a price was paid for these wives! But such are "the wages of sin." (See Num. 31:17 and Deut. 20:13-14 for precedents.)

The elders held another meeting to discuss how they could provide wives for the remaining 200 men. Somebody remembered that many of the virgins from the tribes participated in an annual feast at Shiloh. If the remaining 200 men of Benjamin hid near the place, they could each kidnap a girl and take her home as a wife. The tribes wouldn't be violating their oath because they wouldn't be *giving* the girls as brides. The girls were being *taken*. It was a matter of semantics, but they agreed to follow the plan.

Thus, the 600 men got their brides, the eleven tribes kept their vow, the citizens of Gibeah were punished, the tribe of Benjamin was taught a lesson, and the twelve tribes of Israel were saved. The 600 men of Benjamin, with their brides, returned to their inheritance, cleaned up the debris, repaired the cities, and started life all over again.

But all of this carnage and destruction happened because

one Levite didn't have the courage to stand up for what was right and treat his wife honorably. Once again, as with Jonathan, Micah, and the Danites (Jud. 17–18), the problem started in the home. As goes the home, so goes the nation.

For the fourth time (17:6; 18:1; 19:1), the writer tells us that "there was no king in Israel"; and for the second time (17:6), he adds that "every man did that which was right in his own eyes." Today, there is no king in Israel because the nation chose Barabbas instead of Jesus (Luke 23:13-25). They said, "We will not have this man to reign over us" (Luke 19:14). Because there's no king in Israel, people are rebelling against God and doing whatever pleases them; and it will be that way until the King returns and takes His throne on earth.

But God's people today don't live in the Book of Judges; *they live in the Book of Ruth!*[4] It's difficult to believe that the story narrated in the Book of Ruth takes place in the time of the Judges (Ruth 1:1). The story of Ruth is a *love story* about a man seeking a bride. It's a *redemption story,* about a wealthy man willingly paying the price to purchase his beloved bride and make her his very own. It's a *harvest story* about the Lord of the harvest bringing in the sheaves.

Through faith in Jesus Christ, all of God's people today share in His love. We belong wholly to Him because He redeemed us by His blood when He died for us on the cross. We are laborers together in the harvest. What a wonderful life we have in a world torn apart by sin and selfishness! And what a wonderful privilege we have to share the Good News with others!

In which book are you living—the Book of Judges or the Book of Ruth?

THIRTEEN

DRAWING SOME LESSONS FROM THE BOOK OF JUDGES

Looking Back and Looking Around

As we look back at our studies and look around at our world and God's church, we can draw some conclusions about the Christian life and Christian service and make some applications for our own ministries today.

1. God is looking for servants

He's looking for people who are available to hear His Word, receive His power, and do His will. God can use all kinds of men and women. Like Gideon, some of God's servants are weak in themselves but strong in the Lord. Like Barak, some people don't want to fight the enemy alone. All of us are different, but all of us can serve the Lord for His glory.

If God calls you to serve Him, it's not primarily because of your abilities and talents. He often calls people who seem to have no leadership qualities at all. He calls you because you are yielded to Him and available to do His will. Don't look at yourself; don't look only at the challenge; look to the Lord.

2. God rules and overrules in history

The Book of Judges makes it clear that God can work in and through all nations, Gentiles as well as Jews. God has "determined the times before appointed, and the bounds of their habitation" (Acts 17:26). He's the God of both history and geography. He can use Gentile nations to chasten His own people Israel. He can put one ruler up and bring down another.

While there may not be an obvious *pattern* to history, although historians may search for it, there is definitely a *plan* to history; because God is in control. As Dr. A.T. Pierson used to say, "History is His story." Events that look to us like accidents are really appointments (Rom. 8:28). As dark as the days were in the time of the Judges, God was still on the throne, accomplishing His purposes. This ought to encourage us to trust Him and keep serving Him, no matter how grim the prospects might be in this wicked world.

3. God gives nations the leaders they deserve

I've pointed out several times in these studies that the quality of the character of the judges deteriorated, starting with Gideon. By the time we get to Samson, we see great physical strength wedded to the weakest kind of character. Gideon, Jepthah, and Samson did the work God gave them to do, but they provided no spiritual leadership for the people.

Philosophers have debated for centuries whether or not a bad person can be a good leader. Perhaps the key question is, "What kind of leadership are you talking about?" A general who swears, bullies, lies, and ignores the Word of God, if he's an experienced soldier, can no doubt provide effective leadership for an army; but he won't provide the kind of example that builds character.

All of God's servants are flawed in some way, but that shouldn't be an excuse for us to sin or to do less than our best. We should all strive to build Christian character and to develop our skills to the glory of God. Dedication is no substitute for careless work, but success in the eyes of people is no substitute for likeness to Jesus Christ. Like David, we should serve the Lord with both integrity and skillfulness (Ps. 78:72).

4. God graciously forgives and helps us begin again

The historical cycle in the Book of Judges assures us that God chastens when we disobey and forgives when we repent and confess our sins. It's too bad we don't learn from the failures of others and from our own past failures, but that's one of the occupational hazards of being human.

We must remember that the nation of Israel was in a special covenant relationship with God. He promised to bless them if they obeyed His Law and chasten them if they disobeyed. Nowhere in the New Testament has God promised to make His people's lives today easy and comfortable if they obey the Lord. Jesus lived a perfect life on earth, yet He suffered as no one has ever suffered; and we're called to be like Jesus. Paul was a man devoted to the Lord, yet he experienced innumerable trials.

If we obey the Lord just to get things from Him or to escape from trials, then our relationship to Him isn't very loving. It's more of a "contract" relationship: we'll obey Him if He'll give us what we want. Jesus dealt with this selfish attitude in His Parable of the Laborers (Matt. 20:1-16), which was given in answer to Peter's question, "What shall we have therefore?" (Matt. 19:27)

We should obey the Lord because we love Him. Sometimes obeying Him will lead us into trials, but He will see us through. We need to be like the three Jews who faced the fiery furnace: "Our God whom we serve is able to deliver us from the burning fiery furnace, and He will deliver us from your hand, O King. But if not, let it be known to you, O King, that we do not serve your gods, nor will we worship the golden image which you have set up" (Dan. 3:17-18, NKJV).

5. God's Word stands despite people's unfaithfulness

The judges accomplished what they did because they believed the Word of God (Heb. 11:32-34). Sometimes their faith was weak and imperfect, but God honored their trust and glorified His name through them. But even when the leaders and the people disobeyed Him, their unbelief and disobedience didn't cancel the Word of God.

God's Word never fails. If we obey it, He is faithful to bless us, keep His promises, and accomplish His purposes. If we disobey His will, He is faithful to chasten us and bring us back to the place of submission. The Word doesn't change and God's character doesn't change.

As His children, we live on *promises* and not *explanations*. God doesn't have to explain to us what He's doing or why He's doing it that way. He will always give His servants just the promises they need to get the job done.

6. God uses human government to accomplish His will

There was "no king in Israel," but God was still able to work. Even when there was a king in Israel, it was no guarantee that the people would obey God. Government is important, and God established government; but rulers, senates or parliaments can't limit God.

According to Romans 13, God instituted human government for our good, and it's our responsibility to respect and obey it. We may not respect the people in office, but we must respect the office. God has accomplished His purposes with His people in different kinds of political systems, including monarchies and dictatorships. We mustn't think that He needs a democracy or a constitutional monarchy in order to accomplish His will. God is sovereign!

Regardless of the form of government a nation has, Proverbs 14:34 still applies: "Righteousness exalts a nation, but sin is a reproach to any people" (NKJV).

7. When God's people are unspiritual, the nations decay
Apostasy and anarchy go together. We're the light of the world and the salt of the earth (Matt. 5:13-16), and God wants us to exert a positive influence on society. When the church ceases to be a holy people, obedient to the Lord, the salt loses its taste and the light goes under a bushel. G. Campbell Morgan said that the church did the most for the world when the church was the least like the world. Today, many churches have the idea they must imitate the world in order to reach the world. And they are wrong!

When Israel adopted the lifestyle of the pagan nations around them, they weakened their own nation. When Israel turned to idols, God turned from blessing them. Nations don't decay and collapse because of the people who peddle pornography or narcotics, but because of Christians who are no longer salt and light. God expects sinners to act like sinners, though He disapproves of what they do; but He doesn't expect *saints* to act like sinners. Compromising Christians not only hurt themselves and their families and churches, but also contribute to the decay of the whole nation.

8. God doesn't tell the whole story all at once
We know a good deal about Deborah, Gideon, Jepthah, and Samson, but we don't know much about Shamgar, Tola, and Jair. God hasn't seen fit to put into His Word all the works of all of His servants, yet these people played important roles in accomplishing His purposes.

The people of God may never recognize the work you do for the Lord. You may be a Tola, an Ibzan, or an Elon. Don't be discouraged! God keeps the records and will one day reward you for your faithful service. It's not important that other people see what you do and compliment you on it. It is important that we serve the Lord and seek to please Him.

There's another caution here: Don't be too quick to judge

what other people are doing, and don't get the idea that you're the only one faithfully serving the Lord. During the period of the Judges, different people were serving God in different places, and not all of them knew all that was going on. So it is with the work of God today. In spite of the excellent news coverage in the Christian world, we don't always know what God is doing in and through His servants in various parts of the globe. When we feel discouraged, perhaps we'd be encouraged if we knew the whole story.

"Therefore judge nothing before the time, until the Lord come, who both will bring to light the hidden things of darkness, and will make manifest the counsels of the hearts; and then shall every man have praise of God" (1 Cor. 4:5).

9. God still blesses those who live by faith

It has well been said that faith is not believing in spite of evidence (that's superstition) but obeying in spite of consequence. I might add that it also means obeying God no matter what we see around us or ahead of us or how we feel within us. Faith doesn't depend on our emotions (Gideon was frightened much of the time, and Samson felt he still had his old power) or our understanding of the situation. Faith takes God at His Word and does what He tells us to do.

You can't serve God without faith, because "without faith it is impossible to please Him" (Heb. 11:6). "Whatsoever is not of faith is sin" (Rom. 14:23). If we wait until we have perfect faith, we'll never do much for the Lord. He honors even weak faith and seeks to make it stronger. Exercising faith is like exercising muscles: The more you exercise, the stronger the muscles become.

10. God's story isn't finished yet

I must confess that I occasionally felt depressed as I wrote this book. One day I said to my wife, "I'll be glad when *Be*

Available is finished. There just isn't much good news in the Book of Judges!"

But the Book of Judges isn't the end of the story! In fact, the book begins with the words "now it came to pass," which is a strange way to begin a book. In the Hebrew, it reads "and it was." If I started a book with the phrase "and it was," the editors would send the manuscript back to me and tell me to brush up on my syntax.

But there are eight Old Testament books that begin with "and it was": Joshua, Judges, Ruth, 1 and 2 Samuel, Esther, Ezekiel, and Jonah. Why? *Because they're all part of the continuing story that God is writing!* The end of the Book of Joshua doesn't end the work of God in this world, for the Book of Judges begins with "and it was." The story goes on! God is still working!

If the Book of Judges is the book of "no king," just keep in mind that 2 Samuel is the book of *God's king;* and David takes the throne and brings order and peace to the land. When the outlook is grim, just remind yourself that *God hasn't finished the story yet.*

A friend of mine who's involved in professional basketball likes to watch videos of his team's winning games. Even during the tightest moments of the game, he can relax in front of the TV set *because he already knows how it's going to end.*

There are days when God's people look at a chaotic world, a nation given to greed and violence, and a church weak and divided, and they wonder whether it's worth it all to walk with God and do His will. When that happens, remind yourself that *God's people know how it's going to end!* The Book of Judges isn't the last installment; the Book of Revelation is! And God assures us that righteousness will triumph, evil will be judged, and faith will be rewarded.

No Christian can do everything, but every Christian can do

something, and God will put all these "somethings" together to get His work done in this world.

You never can tell what God has planned for you, so *be available!*

After all, one of these days, you'll have to be accountable, and you'll want to be ready.

ENDNOTES

Chapter 1

1. The references are from Judges 9, 16, 19, 21, and 5:6 (in order).
2. Judges is the book of "no king," 1 Samuel is the book of "man's king" (Saul), and 2 Samuel is the book of "God's king" (David). The world today is living in the Book of Judges because there is no king in Israel. When presented with their rightful King, the Jews said, "We have no king but Caesar." Next on the agenda is the appearance of "man's king" (Antichrist) who will usher in world control and chaos. Then "God's King" will appear, defeat His enemies, and establish His righteous kingdom. Note that the Book of Ruth takes place during the period of the Judges (Ruth 1:1) and that it is a love story and a harvest story. God's people are living in the Book of Ruth, sharing in the harvest and waiting for the wedding.
3. The original name was Kiriath-sepher, which means "city of books." Perhaps it had a large library or it was the "county seat," where official records were deposited.
4. In the Hebrew, the words "brother-in-law" and "father-in-law" use the same letters, which helps explain the problem connected with the names Reuel, Jethro, and Hobab (Ex. 2:18; 3:1; Num. 10:29; Jud. 4:11). Some students think that Moses' father-in-law had two names, Hobab and Jethro, and that Reuel was a distant relative.
5. G. Campbell Morgan, *Living Messages of the Books of the Bible*, vol. 1 (Old Tappan, N.J.: Fleming H. Revell, 1912), 104.
6. This explains why Elijah challenged Baal to send rain (1 Kings 18).
7. God would also use these nations to test Israel (Jud. 2:22) and train the new generation for war (3:1-3). When God isn't allowed to rule, He overrules and accomplishes purposes we never imagined.

Chapter 2

1. We must never think that the wrath of God is like a child's temper tantrum. A holy God must not only hate sin but also hate

what sin does to people. If the police arrest parents for child abuse, what should God have done when His people were sacrificing their children on pagan altars? The English poet Thomas Traherne (c. 1636–74) said, "Love can forbear, and Love can forgive . . . but Love can never be reconciled to an unlovely object. He can never therefore be reconciled to your sin, because sin itself is incapable of being altered; but He may be reconciled to your person, because that may be restored." This explains how God can both hate sin but love the sinner; and even while He is angry at our sins, He chastens us in love "that we might be partakers of His holiness" (Heb. 12:10).

2. The fact that Ehud assassinated a ruler bothers some people, who (for some reason) aren't disturbed that Ehud and his men later slaughtered 10,000 healthy young Moabites (Jud. 3:29). If wars of liberation are justified, then how many of the enemy die is really immaterial, so long as you achieve your goal of freedom. The death rate, however, is still one apiece.

3. King Eglon's name means "little bull calf." Ehud had killed the "fatted calf."

4. Joseph Parker, *The People's Bible*, vol. 5 (London: Hazell, Watson, and Viney, Ltd., 1896), 345.

Chapter 3

1. You would expect Judges 4:1 to read "when Shamgar was dead" since Shamgar is the judge last named. But Shamgar's ministry was local and contemporary with that of Deborah (5:6-7). Meanwhile, Ehud exercised authority over all the land and was the architect of the eighty years of rest.

2. The selection of Deborah may also indicate that, at that time, there were no men willing and able to do the job. Even Barak was afraid to confront the enemy without Deborah's help, and he was a man of faith (Heb. 11:32). For an inspiring account of women of God who have made a difference in the church and the world, see *Daughters of the Church* by Ruth A. Tucker and Walter Liefeld (Zondervan, 1987); and *A Dictionary of Women in Church History* by Mary L. Hammack (Moody Press, 1984).

3. It's possible that this verse is speaking of deception rather than disarmament. Israel might have possessed weapons but kept them hidden from the enemy. When war was declared, the men brought them out.

4. If you were the guest of an Eastern sheik, you were under his protection; and he would not turn you over to your enemies. He would expect the people in his family and his camp to protect you as well.

5. Judah and Simeon aren't mentioned at all in Judges 4–5. Some students think these two tribes may have already been engaged in wars against the Canaanites.

6. Military leaders have called this area one of the greatest battle-fields in the world. Not only did Barak defeat Sisera there, but also Gideon defeated the Midianites there (Jud. 6–7), and the "battle of Armageddon" will be fought there (Rev. 16:12-16; 17:14). King Saul died there (1 Sam. 31), and King Josiah was killed there in a battle he should never have fought (2 Kings 23:28-30).

7. "The Curse of Meroz" in *Selected Sermons of Phillips Brooks*, edited by William Scarlett (New York: E.P. Dutton, 1950), 127.

8. Sisera was killed by Jael, who had given him milk; and his army was defeated because of Deborah, whose name means "bee." Sisera discovered that "the land of milk and honey" could be a dangerous place!

9. David compared a godly leader to the rising sun and the sun shining after the rain (2 Sam. 23:3-4). When leaders obey God, as Deborah and Barak did, there is always the dawning of a new day for their people; and there will be calm and light after the storm. The armies of Israel had been through a storm, but God had given them the victory.

Chapter 4

1. Ninety-six verses are devoted to the last judge, Samson. The first four judges were godly people; but from the time of Gideon, the leaders began to decay until you get to Samson, the most unspiritual of them all. Because the nation wanted freedom from

the enemy without being dedicated to God, they didn't deserve godly leaders. Sometimes God gives His people exactly what they deserve.

2. We usually call Samuel the first of the prophets (Acts 3:24), but there were unnamed prophets before Samuel's time.

3. The most popular image of the local church today is that of the corporation, with the pastor as the CEO. I wonder how many churches would want a CEO with the credentials of some of the people God used in the Bible? Moses was eighty years old when he began his ministry and he was wanted for murder in Egypt. Jacob was a schemer. Elijah suffered from depression, and so did Jeremiah. Hosea couldn't keep his marriage together. Amos, a farmer, had no ministerial training. Peter tried to kill a man with his sword. John Mark was a quitter, and Paul couldn't get along with his associate Barnabas. These traits are not excuses either for leaders to sin or for churches to lower their standards, but they do remind us that God's ways aren't always our ways. The man or woman we think least qualified for God's work may turn out to be a mighty servant of God.

4. A.W. Tozer, *The Knowledge of the Holy* (New York: Harper, 1961), 66.

5. Wherever Abraham journeyed, he built an altar (Gen. 12:7-8; 13:4, 18; 22:9); and Joshua left many monuments of Israel's march of Conquest through the land.

6. Joseph Parker comments: "The least one can do is to give a reformer a nickname. If we may not smite him, we may at least throw some appellation at him which we hope the enemy will take up and use as a sting or a thong" *(The People's Bible, vol. 6, 16)*. But Gideon's achievements transformed a contemptible nickname into an honorable title that he was proud to wear. After all, Jehovah did prove Himself greater than Baal!

7. Joseph Parker defends Gideon when he writes, "Men cannot be courageous all at once" *(The People's Bible, vol. 6, 14)*. But courage comes from faith, and faith doesn't become strong when we ask God to bless our unbelief by performing miracles. The way to grow in faith and courage is to hear God's Word, believe His promises, and obey what He tells us to do. God may stoop to our weakness

once or twice, but He won't permit us to live at that juvenile level all our lives.

Chapter 5

1. G. Campbell Morgan, *The Westminster Pulpit*, vol. 4, 209.
2. My friend, Dr. J. Vernon McGee, used to raise the question, "Why didn't Gideon go home? After all, he was afraid!" Courage isn't necessarily the absence of fear; it's the overcoming of fear by transforming it into power. I once asked a well-known Christian collegiate star quarterback how he was able to run the ball so far down the field, and his reply was, "I was scared, just plain scared; so I kept moving!" There is a fear that paralyzes and a fear that energizes, and Gideon's fear was the latter kind.

Chapter 6

1. Manasseh and Ephraim were both sons of Joseph and grandsons of Jacob. Manasseh was the firstborn, but Jacob reversed their birth order when he blessed them (Gen. 41:50-52; 48:1ff). In fact, he "adopted" the two sons as replacements for Reuben and Simeon (Gen. 48:5; 49:4), and this gave Ephraim prominence in Israel.
2. Ephraim's pride later created problems for Jephthah (Jud. 12:1-6), whose response wasn't as conciliatory as Gideon's!
3. Some expositors think that Gideon made the men lie down naked on the ground, covered them with thorny branches and then drove a threshing sledge over them until they died. This seems a brutal way for him to treat his own brethren, no matter how meanly they had treated him and his men, but it's stated clearly that Gideon killed the rebels in Peniel who had treated him the same way. We must remember, however, that these were cruel times and "every man was doing that which was right in his own eyes."
4. See Pss. 47; 68:24; 74:12; 89:18; 98:6; 145:1; Isa. 6:5; 33:22; 44:6. In their song of praise after passing through the Red Sea at the Exodus, Israel acknowledged Jehovah's kingship when they

sang, "The Lord shall reign forever and ever" (Ex. 15:18).

5. Remember that one of the key themes in the Book of Judges is that there was "no king in Israel" at that time (17:6; 18:1; 19:1; 21:25). The writer seems to want to emphasize the need for a king to correct the political division and spiritual decay of the nation. Later, the people asked Samuel for a king (1 Sam. 8); and God told him to grant their request. Everything Moses and Samuel warned them about their kings did to them, but fallen human nature would rather have visible human leaders instead of the invisible, immortal God of heaven and earth.

6. This is the last time you will find a period of peace mentioned in the Book of Judges. The remaining judges mainly ruled locally, and most of them had short tenures.

Chapter 7

1. If the awful carnage recorded in this chapter upsets you, just be reminded that modern dictators like Idi Amin, Joseph Stalin, and Adolph Hitler have done far worse. Norman Cousins estimated that for every word in Hitler's book *Mein Kampf*, 125 people died in World War II.

2. We must not think that Abimelech reigned supremely over the entire nation. There wasn't that kind of national solidarity during the days of the Judges. It was more like the post-Revolution period in American history when the colonies operated under the Articles of Confederation. Abimelech was in control of Shechem and Beth-Millo ("house of Millo," 9:6, KJV), Arumah (v. 41), and Thebez (v. 50), which suggests that he had direct rule over the western part of Manasseh. Judges 9:22 in the KJV implies that Abimelech actually "reigned" and that "all Israel" submitted to him for three years. But "reigned" is too strong a word; "governed" would be better. "All Israel" (at least, those who knew what had happened) had to acknowledge Abimelech as their ruler, but it's doubtful that his influence reached to all of the tribes.

3. In fairness to Plato and Seneca, it should be pointed out that they were not defending political brutality—the end justifies the

means—but discussing how to bring about justice in society. "Might is right" and "might makes right" only if we sincerely want to do right.

4. Twice we're told that Abimelech killed seventy men (vv. 18, 56), but if Jotham escaped, only sixty-nine were killed. But this is no more an error than are John 20:24 and 1 Cor. 15:5, both of which call the band of disciples "the Twelve" at a time when there were only eleven apostles.

5. Ezekiel 31 and Daniel 4 both use trees to represent leaders or nations.

Chapter 8

1. John F. Kennedy, *Profiles in Courage* (New York: Harper and Brothers, 1955), 245.

2. *The Living Bible* reads "the first person coming out of his house."

3. Baal worship was the prevalent religion among the Canaanites, and it didn't include the sacrifice of children. The Ammonites put their children through the fire as part of their worship of Molech. Eighteen years before, the people of Israel had turned to heathen gods; and for this, the Lord had severely chastened them (10:6-9). It's unthinkable that Jephthah would adopt a heathen practice in order to get God's help when the nation had suffered so greatly for adopting heathen practices! For God to honor such a thing would make the people ask, "If heathen practices are so evil, then why did You send all that suffering?"

4. Even if a priest did offer Jephthah's daughter as a burnt offering, the sacrifice would not be acceptable because the burnt offering had to be a male (Lev. 1:3, 10).

5. If Jephthah were going to kill his daughter, he would want her home with himself and not running around on the mountains with her girlfriends. Furthermore, why would the girl lament her *virginity* if she expected to die? Of what significance is virginity if you're heading for the grave? It seems likely that she would have lamented her impending death instead. Perhaps she was lamenting the fact

that she hadn't married and therefore did not leave her father any grandchildren. But if that were the case, *her father* should have been doing the grieving, because marriages were arranged by the family, not by the individuals involved.

Chapter 9

1. If you still have your college English literature textbook, read John Milton's epic poem "Samson Agonistes" and compare it with the biblical account. Milton presents some insights into the mind and heart of Samson that can help us better understand the impact of his life for good and for evil.

2. Our word "Palestine" comes from the word "Philistine."

3. Leon Wood, *The Distressing Days of the Judges* (Grand Rapids: Zondervan Publishing House, 1975), 302–5.

4. Other servants of God who were chosen before birth include Jeremiah (Jer. 1:4-5) and Paul (Gal. 1:15), although Psalm 139:15-16 teaches that the Lord is involved in the conception of *every* child.

5. "Nazirite" must not be confused with "Nazarene" (Matt. 2:23; 26:71). Since Jesus drank wine (Matt. 11:19; Mark 11:25) and touched dead bodies (Luke 7:14; 8:54), He was obviously not a Nazirite.

6. The phrase "pleases me well" is literally "right in my eyes." It reminds us that during the period of the Judges "every man did that which was right in his own eyes" (17:6; 21:25). Instead of following the Lord, Samson was following the crowd and doing the "in" thing.

7. The week-long wedding feast (14:17) certainly involved wine, and it's probable that Samson drank it. He was the bridegroom and was expected to encourage his guests to enjoy themselves. The word translated "feast" means "a drinking party."

8. There was a form of marriage in which the wife remained with her parents and the husband visited her from time to time. But even if that were the case, the wife would expect her husband to consummate the marriage before going away. Perhaps Samson hoped to do that when he visited her at wheat harvest (15:1-3), but then he learned that she wasn't his wife!

ENDNOTES

Chapter 10

1. No doubt you can think of many more examples from the Scriptures. Lot had the privilege of walking with Abraham and yet ended in a cave, drunk and committing incest with his daughters. King Saul began as a humble man but ended up a suicide, destroyed by his stubborn pride. King Uzziah was a godly man until he became strong. When he tried to usurp the place of the priests, God judged him by giving him leprosy. Ahithophel was David's most trusted advisor, but he ended up hanging himself. Paul's helper Demas abandoned the ministry because he "loved this present world" (2 Tim. 4:10). May the Lord help us all to end well!

2. There are several surprised bridegrooms in the Bible. Adam went to sleep a single man and woke up to learn (happily) that he was married (Gen. 2:21-25). Jacob woke up and discovered he was married to the wrong woman (Gen. 29:21-30). Boaz woke up to find his prospective wife lying at his feet on the threshing floor (Ruth 3:1-13). Life is full of rude awakenings.

3. James Moffatt, *A New Translation of the Bible* (London: Hodder and Stoughton, 1934), 291.

4. Micah offered to pay his household priest ten pieces of silver a year, plus room and board (17:10); so Delilah was being rewarded most generously. If each of the princes of the five Philistine cities was in on the plan, as they probably were, Delilah would have received 5,500 pieces of silver. This shows how important it was to the Philistine leaders that Samson be captured.

5. Judges 16:16 suggests that Samson saw her daily ("day after day," NIV). Whether he traveled to her house every day or simply moved in with her, we aren't told. He was playing the fool, but nobody could convince him of it.

6. The Holy Spirit left King Saul because of his sins (1 Sam. 16:14), and he also lost his crown (2 Sam. 1:10). God wants us to "reign in life" (Rom. 5:17), and we will if we walk in the Spirit and yield ourselves wholly to the Lord. Sin makes slaves out of kings; grace makes kings out of sinners.

7. His eyes had gotten him into trouble (Jud. 14:1-2; 16:1), and the "lust of the eyes" had led him into sin. Had Samson walked by

faith, he would have ended his career in honor, glorifying the Lord.

8. Since the Philistines knew that Samson's long hair had something to do with his great power, why did they allow it to grow again? Probably for two reasons: (1) They wanted him to be strong so they could both use his power and exhibit his feats; and (2) they were sure that his blindness prevented him from being dangerous to them anymore. However, it wasn't the length of his hair but the strength of his dedication to God that brought about the change. The Philistines had no way of knowing that God had restored Samson's strength.

9. The second word—*sahaq*—gives us the name "Isaac," which means "laughter." Both Hebrew words carry the idea of entertaining people by making them laugh. The champion is now a comedian.

10. Only two of Samson's prayers are recorded, one for water (15:18) and this one for strength to pull down the pillars. I've suggested that Samson turned his prison into a sanctuary and talked to the Lord, but his "prison prayers" aren't recorded. It's unfortunate that his final words still evidenced a spirit of revenge rather than a desire to glorify God, but let's not be too hard on a man who was willing to give his life in one last attempt to serve the Lord.

11. Alexander Maclaren, *Expositions of Holy Scripture*, vol. 2 (Grand Rapids: Baker Book House, 1975), 256.

Chapter 11

1. In 18:30, Jonathan is identified as "the son of Gershom, the son of Manasseh," which is impossible since Gershom was a son of Moses and didn't belong to the tribe of Manasseh (Ex. 2:22; 1 Chron. 23:14-15). A Levite would come from the tribe of Levi. The addition of the letter *n (nun* in the Hebrew) to the name "Moses" would change it to "Manasseh." In the Hebrew original, the *nun* is found *above the line,* showing that the letter was added to the text later. Hebrew scholars believe that a scribe, zealous to protect the good name of Moses, changed the text so that there wouldn't be an

idolater in Moses' family. The scribe apparently forgot about Aaron.

2. In writing this, I have no intention of indicting the entire advertising industry. Advertising performs a valuable service when it tells us where to find products and services that we really need. It's when advertisers promote unhealthy desires by creating "images" that appeal to the baser instincts of the human heart that I part company with them. Pride, covetousness, and competition for status aren't the healthiest motivations for people who want to build strong homes or a safe and just society. It's good to have the things that money can buy *if* you don't lose the things that money can't buy.

3. The fact that Jonathan's words came true doesn't absolve either him or the spies from being involved in activities outside the will of God. Jonathan's prophecy came true because the Danites were strong and the people of Laish were weak and unprotected.

4. As serious as their crimes were, I confess I can't help smiling as I envision five brave men stealing gods *that can't even protect themselves!* The Scriptures that come to mind are Isaiah 40:18-31 and 44:9-20, as well as Psalm 115.

5. However serious the present crime rate may be in the United States, let's not so idealize the past that we get things out of proportion. See *Our Violent Past* by Irving J. Sloan (New York: Random House, 1970). Violence is rooted in the human heart (Gen. 6:5, 11-12), and only the grace of God can remove it.

6. Bible students aren't agreed as to which "captivity" is meant in Judges 18:30. If it refers to the Assyrian Captivity of the Northern Kingdom in 722 B.C., then an editor had to add these words to the text at a later date. But the frequent phrase "no king in Israel" suggests that *Judges* was written during the early days of the monarchy, centuries away from the Assyrian invasion. This captivity may have been the invasion of the Philistines or perhaps some local war about which we have no information. Jonathan probably married a girl from the tribe of Dan, and his sons continued the false priesthood that he had started, but we don't know for how long. If we knew, we could determine the date of the "captivity."

BE AVAILABLE

Chapter 12

1. King Saul used a similar approach to arouse the people to fight the Ammonites, but he cut up a yoke of oxen (1 Sam. 11:1-7). The sin of Gibeah was so terrible that the Prophet Hosea referred to it centuries later as an example of great sin (Hosea 9:9 and 10:9).

2. Keep in mind that this event took place early in the period of the Judges, at a time when the nation wasn't under foreign oppression. Though they had no central government, the tribes were still united and able to muster troops and wage war together.

3. Some expositors think that they went to the city of Bethel, since "house of God" in the Hebrew is *beth-elohim* and not *bethel*. See also 20:26. The tabernacle was moved from place to place. It was first located in Shechem (Josh. 8:30-35), and then was moved to Shiloh (Josh. 18:1 and 22:12; Jud. 18:31). At one time it was at Nob (1 Sam. 21) and also Gibeon (1 Chron. 16:39; 21:29), not to be confused with Gibeah.

4. For an exposition of the Book of Ruth, see my book *Be Committed,* which deals with the Book of Ruth and the Book of Esther. It's published by Victor Books, Wheaton, Illinois.

Be Alive (John 1—12)

by Warren W. Wiersbe

'The profoundest book in the world'.

As he studied and wrote this book, Dr Warren W. Wiersbe 'felt like a man standing on holy ground.' For he realised all the more the truth of the statement of the great Greek scholar Dr A. T. Robertson: "The Gospel of John is 'the profoundest book in the world.' "

In *BE ALIVE* Dr Wiersbe presents basic teachings of the first 12 chapters of John's Gospel with his unique outline and style. He urges readers to approach its truth with hearts and minds of worshippers.

Come to know the living Saviour better and *BE ALIVE*

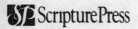 Scripture Press

Be Satisfied (Ecclesiastes)

by Warren W. Wiersbe

Learn to enjoy life amid its uncertainties.

'To every thing there is a season, and a time to every purpose under heaven' (Eccles 3:1). King Solomon had every opportunity to examine life and ponder its mysteries and perplexities. He faced the same issues that we all confront daily:

▶ The seeming monotony of life.
▶ The vanity of wisdom.
▶ The futility of wealth.
▶ The certainty of death.

Ecclesiastes is an inspired road map that guides you through the puzzles and problems of living and shows you the source by which you too may *Be Satisfied*.

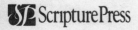

Scripture Press

Be Rich (Ephesians)

by Warren W. Wiersbe

Want wealth that won't vanish? The cost of living
index frightens most of us. Prices go up, up, up. The
value of money goes down, down, down. Earthly
wealth seems more and more transient. But *BE RICH*
tells you where to find wealth that can change your
life, and change your attitude towards things that the
world calls riches. *BE RICH* brings you:

- A study of the Christian home and the work of the
  Holy Spirit
- A study of the strategy of Satan, and how
  Christians can be victorious
- A study of each Christian's responsibility in the
  light of his great wealth in Christ.

  ... 'You can truly' *BE RICH*

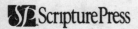
ScripturePress

BE COMMITTED
Ruth & Esther

Dr Warren W. Wiersbe

When you are tempted to compromise or quit...

think of Ruth and Esther, two Old Testament heroines of the faith. Singled out as the only women to have Bible books named after them, Ruth and Esther lived in very different worlds, one a poor peasant and the other a powerful queen. Yet both dared to do the right thing when confronted with the easyway out, and God rewarded them for their courage and commitment.

As you study the books of Ruth and Esther, you will appreciate anew the tough choices of faith these women made, and you will be encouraged to do the same as you rely on the God who accomplishes His purposes through people who trust Him.

Dr Warren W. Wiersbe is an author, pastor, and radio Bible teacher. He was pastor of Chicago's Moody Memorial Church and most recently served as General Director of Back to the Bible. He has authored over 105 books, including the New Testament 'BE' Series.

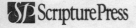
ScripturePress